# 1971

1982

1989

# SINCE THE WORLD BEGAN

## WALT DISNEY WORLD® THE FIRST 25 YEARS

BY JEFF KURTTI
FOREWORD BY ROY E. DISNEY

A ROUNDTABLE PRESS BOOK
HYPERION
NEW YORK

*"Only you yourself matter, your friends matter, good books matter."*

—TATYANA TOLSTAYA

THIS BOOK IS DEDICATED TO PAUL WOLSKI

With my enduring affection, respect, and gratitude.

*". . . how rare it is to be able to get into that kind of conversation with a friend that goes on for years and years and just continues underneath everything . . . "*

—MARGE PIERCY



A Roundtable Press Book


Printed in the United States of America.
For information, address Hyperion, 114 Fifth Avenue, New York, NY 10011.



PHOTOGRAPH PAGE 1:
Cinderella Castle in the Magic Kingdom, opened in 1971

PHOTOGRAPH PAGE 2:
Spaceship Earth in EPCOT Center, opened in 1982

PHOTOGRAPH PAGE 3:
Grauman's Chinese Theater at Disney-MGM Studios, opened in 1989

PHOTOGRAPH PAGE 4:
Opening day in 1971 at Walt Disney World

FOR ROUNDTABLE PRESS
Directors: Susan E. Meyer, Marsha Melnick
Executive Editor: Amy T. Jonak
Editors: Carol Spier, Sue Heinemann
Photo Editor/Consultant: Steven Rosen
Assistant Editor: Abigail Anderson
Design: Nai Y. Chang
Production: Bill Rose

FOR HYPERION
Editor: Wendy Lefkon
Editorial Assistant: Monique Peterson

Library of Congress Cataloging-in-Publication Data
Kurtti, Jeff.
Since the world began : Walt Disney World, the first 25 years / by Jeff Kurtti ; foreword by Roy E. Disney. — 1st ed.
p. cm.
Includes bibliographical references.
ISBN 0-7868-6248-3 (hc). — ISBN 0-7868-8219-0 (pbk.)
1. Walt Disney World (Fla.)—History. I. Title.
GV1853.3.F62W3455 1996
791'.06'875924—dc20 96-23099
CIP

First Edition
4 6 8 10 9 7 5 3

# CONTENTS

Walt Disney World

## FOREWORD

It's difficult to believe it has been 25 years since my father, Roy O. Disney, officially dedicated Walt Disney World. The lives of my entire family were forever altered more than 30 years ago, when my Uncle Walt passed away and my father—who was about to retire—decided to put off his plans and see to it that his brother's dream became a reality.

My father and Walt had a very distinct way of working together—Walt was the creative genius always in the public eye; Roy handled business and finance matters behind the scenes; and they rarely if ever crossed that line. Suddenly, in 1966, my dad had to venture into the creative decision-making process—a position where he was admittedly less than comfortable. As I imagine you all agree, he more than rose to the occasion. Seeing Walt Disney World open allowed him both to fulfill a promise to his brother and to pay an enormous tribute to him by naming the new resort "Walt Disney World" instead of Walt's previously planned "Disney World."

When my father dedicated the theme park he said: "May Walt Disney World bring joy and inspiration and new knowledge to all who come to this happy place—a Magic Kingdom where the young at heart of all ages can laugh and play and learn together."

I'll never forget opening day. As I stood at the Walt Disney World railroad station with my wife, Patty; our children, Roy, Susan, Abby, and Tim; my mother; and my Aunt Lilly—and the band (76 trombones, 110 cornets, and the rest, led by Meredith Willson) came marching in—the entire platform began to throb with the music. It was a moment of pride and sentiment that I'll always cherish.

When all is said and done, the admiration I have for my father and what he had to force himself to do is simply endless. Ironically, Walt Disney World turned out to be his last labor of love. He died just about two months after opening day.

Aside from the obvious pleasures to be enjoyed at Walt Disney World, my emotional attachment to the resort never fades. On my many trips to Florida each year, I still feel the warmth and charm of the place and, perhaps most importantly, a great bond with my dad. That's why I am delighted to introduce this silver anniversary volume celebrating a place so magical it continues to entertain, educate, and inspire all who visit.

Roy E. Disney
Los Angeles
1996

*Roy Edward Disney, vice chairman of The Walt Disney Company.*

OPPOSITE:
*Mickey Mouse hats keep coming at a merchandise warehouse.*

INTRODUCTION

Like most of the modern-day human race, I grew up with Disney. For me, it was more than a few toys or picture books or a movie that the family went to see. From the time I was five years old, Disney was a hobby, an avocation, sometimes an obsession. Disney was (and is) a part of my life. Its characters and products enthrall me; its history fascinates me; its cultural power awes me.

There was nothing in my life that made me feel so connected to the world. Through the mythology of Disney, I learned that, although not necessarily accepted, the outcast was usually superior. Through Disney's introduction, via television and theme park, I learned about the American West, pirates, futurism and technology, even the paranormal. Disney offered easy entree to a variety of subjects, and although many pundits and educators decry the "Disneyfication" of history, science, and mythology, I would never have made it through ninth-grade algebra without *Donald in Mathmagic Land* or cared about science class without *Our Friend the Atom* and *The Restless Sea.* And not *just* because these films were executed with the skill of showmanship that made their subjects more accessible or entertaining—but also because they were *Disney.*

Like a lot of kids my age in the mid-1960s, the vague information that Disney was doing something big—*really* big—in central Florida was as exciting to anticipate as Christmas. By this time I was a true "Disney geek." I hung on every word I heard, and every scrap I could find on the subject of Disney. (I even learned about Benjamin Disraeli because his encyclopedia entry was next to Walt Disney's.) To this nine-year-old, if "Walt Disney World" was simply a bigger, better Disneyland, that would be fine. But the photographs, television coverage, and Disney publicity painted a preadolescent's picture of a virtual paradise on earth—and I couldn't wait to go.

My dream visit to Walt Disney World didn't occur until 1987, when I had actually become a Disney employee. Far from being a disappointment, finally being at Walt Disney World was like opening the biggest, best Christmas present ever—after a 15-year-long Christmas Eve. As I sat in the Top of the World Lounge at the Contemporary Resort, looking out at the night-lit Magic Kingdom, I realized that the ability to appreciate the resort as an adult—while still maintaining an inventory of mental images and anticipation formed in childhood—gave me the most satisfying first visit possible. Since then, I have returned to Walt Disney World dozens of times, and although my perceptions change from visit to visit, I never cease to wonder how the thing ever got built in the first place.

That's where this book begins. How did a central Florida swamp become the Number One family vacation destination in the world? Whose idea was it? Who built it? Why did they build it there? What were the events and who were the people that inspired its ideas, design, topography, attractions, landscaping, resorts—its very existence? What has it come to mean? What is it going to become?

I hope to shed some light on the foregoing questions. It would be impossible to tell the *complete* story of Walt Disney World in a single volume, but at least I'll tell a *comprehensive* story of Walt Disney World. I hope that you find not only a history but also a sense of the vision and wonder, the artistry, craftsmanship, and storytelling, and the plain fun at the heart of this amazing place, which make it perpetually appealing to millions of visitors every year.

Jeff Kurtti
Los Angeles
February 1996

## A NOTE ON NOMENCLATURE

The text occasionally refers to Walt Disney with the familiar "Walt." This reference is not meant with disrespect, nor to infer some special connection between the author and Walt Disney. It is simply the most efficient way to refer to Walt Disney the person, as opposed to Disney, the corporate entity. It is also interesting to note that during his lifetime, Walt insisted on being called by his first name by all his employees.

From its founding on October 16, 1923, until February 6, 1986, the official name of the Disney organization was "Walt Disney Productions." The name was changed to "The Walt Disney Company" to reflect the more diverse nature of the Disney product and projects.

The Magic Kingdom is, and always has been, the name of the Disneyland-style theme park that was the cornerstone of the original Walt Disney World Phase One development. Although Disneyland is also sometimes secondarily called "Walt Disney's Magic Kingdom," that has never been Disneyland's "official" name. (Also, "The Happiest Place on Earth" is used as a secondary reference *only* to Disneyland.) The term "Walt Disney World" has always applied to the overall Florida property and not specifically to the theme park component of the property.

The application of the term "EPCOT" varies in the text, depending on its use. "EPCOT" was an acronym for "Experimental Prototype Community of Tomorrow," coined by Walt Disney. In the 1970s, when this concept was redeveloped into a theme park, the official nomenclature was changed to "EPCOT Center," to reflect that park's role as the "theme center" of Walt Disney World. In 1994 the name of the park was changed, dropping the word "Center," reducing the acronym to an initial-cap-and-lowercase word, and adding the current year (e.g., "Epcot 96"), to reflect both the overall acceptance of the term "Epcot" and the ever-changing nature of the material the park showcases.

"Disney-MGM Studios Theme Park" was the official name of the third theme park at Walt Disney World from 1989 until 1994. The "Theme Park" reference was dropped in 1994, because by then the public had become familiar with the attraction, and it really didn't apply to the project overall, unnecessarily implying a separation between the park and the production facilities.

SECTION THRU EPCOT
EPCOT

# CHAPTER ONE

# WALT DISNEY'S WORLD

*I am interested in entertaining people, in bringing pleasure, particularly laughter, to others, rather than being concerned with "expressing" myself with obscure creative expressions.*

— WALT DISNEY

On May 4, 1965, a newspaper article appeared in the *Orlando Sentinel*, the local journal of a small central Florida farming community. Two real estate transactions totaling nearly $1.5 million had been recorded in the Osceola county clerk's office, for property totaling slightly more than 9,000 acres. Two smaller sales had been recorded in the same vicinity earlier. Rumors began to surface about the quiet acquisition of large acreage. (The article noted the "consistent rumor" that Walt Disney was buying the land for an "East Coast Disneyland." The rumor faded and subsequently vanished from "plausible" accounts of the land acquisition events.)

During the next month, dozens of tracts of land near Orlando and the Orange–Osceola County border changed hands. The purchasers were listed as Reedy Creek Ranch Corporation, Latin-American Development and Management Corporation, Bay Lake Properties, Inc., and other, unidentified buyers. Speculation ran rampant as to what the "mystery industry" behind the large-scale land purchase might be. Because of the proximity of the properties to Cape Canaveral and the Kennedy Space Center, aerospace industrial firms were believed likely buyers. McDonnell Aircraft, Republic Aviation, Douglas Aviation, and Lockheed were discussed in the press. Hercules Powder Company, Ford, Volkswagen, Chrysler, and Philco were all mentioned. David Rockefeller and Howard Hughes were considered possible buyers. And Disney still popped up every now and then.

# "ALL OF THIS IS WALT DISNEY"

Walt Disney recognized that the name he was given at birth had become one of the most powerful brand names in the entire world. Late in his life, he reportedly said, "*I'm* not Walt Disney anymore. All of *this* is Walt Disney." In the years since his death, this rings even more true. The continuing growth of the Disney entertainment empire has only increased the power of the Disney brand name.

The influence of Walt Disney on 20th-century culture has been far-reaching. The enterprises that benefited directly from the creativity of this remarkable modern genius are manifold: the first synchronized sound cartoon, the first Technicolor® cartoon, the first feature-length animated cartoon, the first use of stereophonic sound in film exhibition, and the complete reinvention of outdoor entertainment are only a few of Walt Disney's innovations. In storytelling, Disney brought a distinct definition—cynics might say a dubious proprietary claim—to dozens of time-honored and beloved stories, while supervising the creation of a cadre of the most beloved fictional characters in human history.

In abstract, Walt Disney's great talent was that of an instinctive storyteller. His colleagues still relate Walt's intuitive feats of knowing precisely how to add, alter, delete, or amend to overcome a story difficulty. The other side of Walt Disney was that of the inveterate tinkerer, a nascent "techno-phile," fascinated by the opportunities offered in the rapidly accelerating technological developments of the 20th century. Philosophically, he was both a product and a reflection of his times. The combinations of these elements contributed to the revolution of family entertainment during Walt Disney's lifetime.

It is important to understand the principles of Walt Disney's character and calling in order to grasp the foundation of the Florida project. The fundamentals of Walt Disney World were established as a distinctive and immeasurably personal statement of the character, talents, hopes, aspirations, and encompassing worldview of Walt Disney.

On a physical level, Disneyland was probably the true starting point of the Walt Disney World project. In Disneyland, Walt was almost immediately confronted with the urban design problems of the park periphery and, as a design aesthete, was horrified by its lack of cohesion. More than that, he seems to have been mystified that those who fed off the guests of Disneyland did not follow the aesthetic and planning precedent of Disneyland in their endeavors.

Walt was continually approached about doing another amusement park, a "replica Disneyland," in another part of the country. He discussed projects or looked at proposed sites in St. Louis, Niagara Falls, Baltimore, Washington, D.C., southern Florida, and Queens, New York.

But Walt wanted more than a second amusement park. He approached sequels to his films uneasily and then only if there was an interesting new story to be told. He had built Disneyland against all odds and in the face of derisive skeptics. Now that its success, as well as the success of other atypical Disney projects, had granted him a large degree of respectability and financial clout, there was no thought of mere repetition.

For central Florida's residents, the land acquisition would mean a huge economic boost for the sleepy scrub forests, swamps, groves, and grazing lands around Orlando. With so much at stake, the watertight confidentiality of the transactions was surprising. Editorials in the Orlando newspapers revealed skillful media management by the brokers and buyer, as well as the cooperation of local press in suppressing what they might know or find out.

## THE MYSTERY UNFOLDS

At the end of June 1965 the *Orlando Evening Star* carried a story announcing the completion of "Phase One" of the mystery project, the land acquisition. The *Star* tallied the sale of 27,258 acres, purchased for a total of $5,018,770. Some of the smallest parcels of land had been the most difficult to obtain—several had been sold by mail in 1911, and many who had inherited these tiny plots didn't even know they owned them. On one of the largest purchases, the mineral rights for the property had already been sold to Tufts University. The purchaser had to retrieve these rights, which added six dollars per acre to the price of the land.

On October 17 the *Orlando Sentinel* ran an article by reporter Emily Bavar, who deduced that the buyer was Walt Disney. A more fully documented piece ran in the *Sentinel* the following Thursday. Official announcement of the project by Florida governor Haydon Burns had been scheduled for November 15, 1965, in Orlando, but he confirmed the rumors on October 25 in Miami. It was time to let everyone know: the mystery industry would be show business; its captain would be Walt Disney.

On November 15, 1965, Governor Burns, flanked on either side by Walt and Roy O. Disney, held a second press conference to elaborate on the October 25 announcement of the new Disney World. The conference itself was a cavalcade of vagaries and generalizations. Two 20-minute films, *The*

'Tis a Privilege to Live in Central Florida
City To Become Hub For Millions Of Tourists, Billions Of Dollars
'e Say: 'Mystery' Industry Is Disne
City Housing 10,000 People Will Be Built
Disneyland—California
AL FLORIDA

*Various newspaper clippings, including the* Orlando Sentinel *article of October 24, 1965, speculating that Disney is behind the "mystery" Florida project.*

Failure Learned
'Tis a Privilege to Live in Central Florida
Orlando, Florida, Tuesday, November 16, 1965
Facility To Employ 4,000 May Be Ready In 3 Years
Disney Tells Of $100 Million Project
Exact Nature Of Attractions To Be Decided
By ELVIS LANE

Walt Di
Tourist

*The November 16, 1965, issue of the* Orlando Sentinel *reports on the second press conference on the new Disney project. The photo shows, from left to right, Walt Disney, Governor Haydon Burns, and Roy O. Disney.*

## THE 1964–65 NEW YORK WORLD'S FAIR

The 1964–65 New York World's Fair is as fundamental to the Walt Disney World story as Disneyland.

Held on the same site as the 1939–40 New York World's Fair, on Flushing Meadows in the borough of Queens, the 1964–65 fair was masterminded by the legendary city planner Robert Moses. With its overt emphasis on commerce and technology, the fair was criticized for its commercialism, lack of originality, and sociopolitical conservatism. In hindsight the 1964–65 New York World's Fair was a charming microcosm of an optimistic America on the verge of social upheaval, a culture perched on the precipice of a new, postindustrial society.

At the fair Walt Disney was able to address many of his personal interests and the fields of endeavor in which he wished to guide his company. On its simplest examination, Walt Disney's involvement in the fair enabled him to build the latest—and most expensive—theme park attractions with the enthusiastic funding of other companies. These attractions were later used in Disneyland and ultimately in Walt Disney World.

Even the name of General Electric Progressland showed its connection to Disney showmanship. For this pavilion, Disney Imagineers developed a unique carousel theater technology, in which a 250-seat theater revolved around a central stage. Carousel of Progress depicted a typical American family from 1880 to 1965 and the positive influence of electricity and home electrical appliances on their lives.

Walt Disney's Magic Skyway was the central experience of the Ford Wonder Rotunda. One of several Disney-designed exhibits in the rotunda, the Magic Skyway used a prototype WEDway PeopleMover technology to propel guests in real Ford convertibles through an Audio-Animatronics® time trip from the Jurassic period to a futuristic Space City.

Great Moments with Mr. Lincoln was the featured attraction of the State of Illinois Pavilion. Robert Moses was so impressed with the Abraham Lincoln figure already being developed by Disney that he convinced Illinois to sponsor the show and in this way prompted Disney to accelerate the development of its Audio-Animatronics technology. In the resulting show a lifelike figure of the 16th U.S. president recited excerpts from Lincoln's letters and speeches.

It's a Small World was the whimsical centerpiece of the UNICEF pavilion. With only nine months until the fair's opening, Walt Disney was approached to design the pavilion. Even though his staff was working day and night on the other three fair shows, Walt accepted the challenge, and the Imagineers formulated what would come to be their most beloved and successful attraction. Richard and Robert Sherman, Academy Award® winners for their work on *Mary Poppins*, contributed the now-famous anthem.

The shows at the fair created not only an opportunity, but a *need* to push the boundaries of the theme park design and engineering techniques that were only in their infancy at Disneyland. Part of each of these shows' complex design involved the extensive use of Disney's proprietary Audio-Animatronics technology, which had debuted on a much smaller scale in Walt Disney's Enchanted Tiki Room at Disneyland in June 1963. New ideas, from crowd control to kinetic sculpture, were given a "baptism by fire" at the New York World's Fair—and the lessons learned there would be used time and time again, in every subsequent Disney park project.

Unknown to almost all but his closest associates at the time, Walt Disney was also tacitly testing whether the Disneyland style of entertainment would "play" on the East Coast. As surprising as it may seem today, many were still uncertain whether Disneyland was just a California anomaly—successful in its context, but unsuited for export to other parts of the country.

Finally, each of the Disney shows in the fair contained an example of technological advance, whether blatantly stated in its show content (Carousel of Progress) or integrated into the presentation (Great Moments with Mr. Lincoln). To Walt Disney, technology *was* the future, and the idea of new technology on display would be played out in Walt's EPCOT concept and the theme park that was ultimately developed from this concept.

Ninety-one percent of the guests at the 1964–65 New York World's Fair attended at least one of the Disney shows. And although critics scoffed at Disney's creations, their popularity convinced many in the Disney organization that the theme park concept was fundamentally reliable, regardless of geographic location.

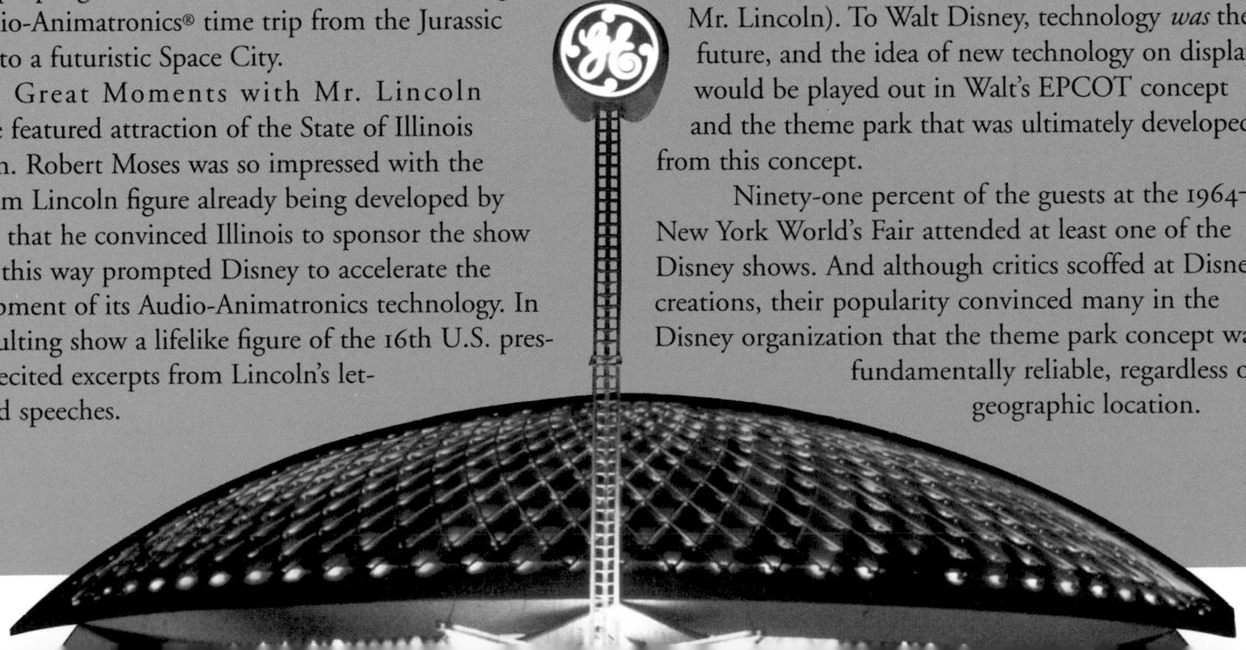

*Disney Image* and *The Economic Impact of Disneyland,* were shown, helping to promote a positive image for the company. But until the cooperation of various state and county bodies could be secured and delineated, there was very little to talk about. Walt commented during the conference that until these agreements were finalized, there was little use in disclosing his ideas.

Few people knew the extent of research that had already been conducted regarding the newly announced site. As early as 1961, potential locations nationwide were being examined and eliminated by Walt Disney and his lieutenants. Studies of the attendance patterns at Disneyland revealed that building near a major population center with a desirable climate had been a key factor in establishing year-round operation.

The problem was, no site presented the perfect combination: a population center, an agreeable climate, *and* the quantity of property that Walt wanted to prevent the urban blight of Disneyland's periphery. Continuing study of the promising areas of the American Southeast revealed that any theme park would have to be designed as a destination, around which a visitor might plan an entire vacation, rather than a day trip (as Disneyland was for many California resident visitors).

The Orlando site offered several attractive qualities. It was adjacent to a growing population center, fed in part by the high-tech and aerospace industries serving the Kennedy Space Center, about 60 miles east. It was near the intersection of several existing federal and interstate highways, which in turn connected the site with three other important roadway systems. Orlando was still a fairly sleepy community, which made land readily available, in great quantity and reasonably priced. The property itself was ordinary enough to be a blank page and simultaneously exotic enough to be picturesque and interesting.

Indeed, much of Walt's initial plan for his project was fairly firmly in place at the time of the November press conference—he just wasn't talking.

*The Florida property in 1965.*

*Many people thought that Disney was simply building "another Disneyland" in Florida, so a great deal of communication was needed to explain what was then called Disney World. Prepared in October 1966, "the EPCOT film" is a 25-minute summary that helped form the background for Walt's primary goal—EPCOT. Written by Marty Sklar (now president of Walt Disney Imagineering), hosted by the familiar, affable, and noticeably excited Walt Disney, it was copiously illustrated with maps, concept renderings, and animation. The EPCOT film was created specifically for employees of Walt Disney Productions, the Florida state legislature, Florida residents, and leaders of American industry; it has never been shown to the general public.*

*An early model of the northwest area of the Walt Disney World Resort property from the southeast, over Seven Seas Lagoon, shows the Magic Kingdom in the left background and the Contemporary Resort in the center background. The A-frame structure in the left background is a proposed "Asian Hotel," announced for the first five-year development phase but never built.*

## THE MASTER PLAN

Walt Disney's vision of Florida's Disney World, as it was then known, included many of the resort amenities familiar to Walt Disney World visitors today. He knew that a basic tourism and group travel business would be needed to give the entire effort a solid fiscal foundation. The Magic Kingdom, much like Disneyland in California, would serve as a focal point for the public. Unlike its Anaheim predecessor, though, the Florida park would feature a surrounding resort community, carefully designed and supervised by the Disney staff. No tawdry motels or neon-lit asphalt strips would sully the Disney image in Florida. No distracting advertising, no aesthetic contradiction, no paving over of everything green would happen on the Disney watch.

Instead, visitors would initially be drawn to visit by the anticipated Disneyland-like amusement park and then discover the variety of unexpected resort amenities. Themed hotels would girdle the outside of the park near a sparkling man-made lagoon. Swimming, boating, sailing, and other water recreation activities would be available. Stables and bridle trails, campgrounds and golf courses, nature tours and nightclubs were all supplementary activities in the proposed vacation kingdom.

Walt Disney's vision extended even farther. An airport on the Osceola County side of the Florida property, a thousand-acre industrial park, and an entrance complex for the entire property just north of the county dividing line were part of Walt's big dream.

Walt's favorite component of the Disney World plan was an entire model city, a seemingly science fiction city of the future. "The most exciting, and by far the most important part of our Florida project," Walt explained in 1966, "in fact, the heart of everything we'll be doing in Disney World—will be our Experimental Prototype Community of Tomorrow. We call it EPCOT. EPCOT will take its cues from the new ideas and new technologies that are now emerging from the creative centers of American industry. It will be a community of tomorrow that will never be completed, but will always be introducing and demonstrating and testing new materials and new systems. And EPCOT will always be a showcase to the world for the ingenuity and imagination of American free enterprise."

## CLEARING THE WAY

There was much work to be done before even the simplest of these ideas could be enacted. Reels of red tape had to be unspooled and cut. Reams of paper had to pass through hundreds of offices. Millions of cubic feet of earth had to be moved. Oceans of water had to course through the 27,000-acre property.

A package of political requirements was prepared to establish independent governing district status for the Disney project. Three acts were proposed and presented to Florida legislators between 1965 and 1967 to

# THE PLANNED CITY

When Walt Disney began dreaming of a "planned city" for his Florida project, he joined a line of noble visionaries including Plato, Francis Bacon, Samuel Butler, Lewis Mumford, and Sir Thomas More, all of whom dreamed of an ideal society in which the social, economic, and environmental evils that plague humankind are eradicated, and the society functions for the good of all. In his writings, More referred to this dream as utopia (Greek for "no place").

In Europe and the United States, utopian visions have often taken the form of experimental communities. Examples included Robert Owen's cooperative communities in New Lanark, Scotland, and New Harmony, Indiana, as well as the Oneida Community in New York State.

Another manifestation of utopian vision was in city planning, where this idealistic approach resulted in the design of "new towns." At the turn of the last century, Sir Ebenezer Howard began the British garden city movement, which attempted to demonstrate that workers could be as efficiently housed in pleasant, unpolluted, verdant environments as in traditional slums. Two of these early garden cities were the 1903 development of Letchworth and the 1920 Welwyn Garden City. The British initiated a torrent of new town development after the Second World War, and constructed 28 meticulously planned new towns, many with their own industries. These towns housed a population in the millions around greater London, Birmingham, Manchester, and other urban areas. All were accompanied by extensive regional and environmental planning.

After World War II, France also developed a national plan for new towns, in order to keep the metropolitan Paris region from becoming overwhelmed by rapid population growth. Half a dozen new town sites were delineated and established around Paris, Grenoble, and Rouen. In 1987 the site of Disneyland Paris was located on a previously established new town site in Marne-la-Vallée, France, 15 miles southeast of Paris.

The United States has had less success with new towns. Experiments in New Harmony and the Oneida Community didn't last beyond the 19th century. Reston, Virginia, and Columbia, Maryland, conceived as "self-sufficient communities," were begun in the 1960s, and real estate development after World War II has included hundreds of bedroom communities, such as Irvine, California (near Los Angeles), Jonathan, Minnesota (near Minneapolis), and Deer Park, Illinois (near Chicago), but these were essentially satellites for the after-hours escape of the upper middle class and did nothing to address the problems of cities. In 1970 the federal Urban Growth and New Community Development Act offered loan guarantees for developers of new towns, provided that the insured project contain a component of low-income housing. Within a decade, all 13 of the UG&NCDA-sponsored projects had failed and been placed in receivership.

Walt Disney's plans for Florida called for an entirely new metropolitan construction. "I don't believe there's a challenge anywhere in the world that's more important to people everywhere than finding solutions to the problems of our cities," Walt said in 1966. "But where do we begin? How do we start answering this great challenge? Well, we're convinced we must start with the public need, and the need is not just for curing the old ills of the old cities—we think the need is for starting from scratch on virgin land and building a special kind of new community. So, that's what EPCOT is: an Experimental Prototype Community that will always be in a state of becoming. It will never cease to be a living blueprint of the future, where people actually live a life they can't find anywhere else in the world. Everything at EPCOT will be dedicated to the happiness of the people who live, work and play here—and those who come here from around the world to visit our living showcase." Not surprisingly, Walt's vision for the Florida property's planned city was dubbed "Waltopia" by Marty Sklar (currently vice chairman of Walt Disney Imagineering).

In the late 1980s The Walt Disney Company began the realization of much that had been included in Walt Disney's original vision of EPCOT. The first phase of this new utopia, called Celebration, was given a 1996 opening date.

## WALT DISNEY'S DEATH

During 1966 Walt Disney's friends and associates began to notice changes in his appearance and behavior. His once-tireless energy flagged; his dapper appearance began to look haggard. A polo injury from the 1930s continued to trouble him. A chronic sinus problem, pneumonia, and a kidney ailment also plagued his 64th year. According to Disney biographer Bob Thomas, "His desk calendar for 1966 shows a series of hospital visits and doctor appointments."

On Wednesday, November 2, 1966, Walt Disney visited St. Joseph's Hospital, across the street from the Disney Studio, for tests. His X-rays revealed a spot on his left lung, and surgery was scheduled for the following Monday. The result was grim. Walt's left lung was cancerous and had to be removed, and the surgeon's prognosis was dire. Disney spent two weeks in recovery at the hospital and returned to work briefly in late November, but the failure of Walt's health was even faster than predicted. He returned to St. Joseph's on November 30, and he died there on December 15, 1966, just 10 days after his 65th birthday.

The reaction from colleagues and the public was instantaneous and poignant. The influence of Walt Disney's work can be seen in the outpouring of grief and sympathy around the world at the time of his death. Writers, actors, artists, princes, kings, and presidents shared in the loss. Journalist Eric Sevareid delivered an eloquent eulogy on television. "He was an original; not just an American original, but an original, period," Sevareid said. "He was a happy accident; one of the happiest this century has experienced; and judging by the way it's been behaving in spite of all Disney tried to tell it about laughter, love, children, puppies and sunrises, the century hardly deserved him."

*"Partners," a magnificent bronze statue by longtime Disney sculptor Blaine Gibson, memorializes Walt Disney with his lifelong partner, Mickey Mouse. There are two of these statues: one at Disneyland and the one shown above, at Walt Disney World.*

define the authority of the Reedy Creek Improvement District, a quasi-governmental entity with power to regulate water management, fire protection, wildlife preservation, roads and bridges, zoning, and building codes within the Disney property. Two municipalities, Bay Lake on the north and Reedy Creek (now Lake Buena Vista) on the east, with their own charters, would be established.

Initial site preparation, horticultural studies, drainage and land reclamation, wildlife management, water storage, and environmental impact studies began. The Disney team spent the year following the press announcement planning, engineering, designing, and gearing up. Walt spent the year solidifying and codifying his creative vision to fit the natural boundaries of the Florida property. He even arrived at an October 1966 meeting with a sketch. It was a footprint of the Florida property, with Walt's own indication of locations for the theme park, resort hotels, lake, campgrounds, and the like. This drawing by Walt Disney, dubbed "Seventh Preliminary Master Plot Plan" by the designers, remained the rudimentary model for the layout of Walt Disney World.

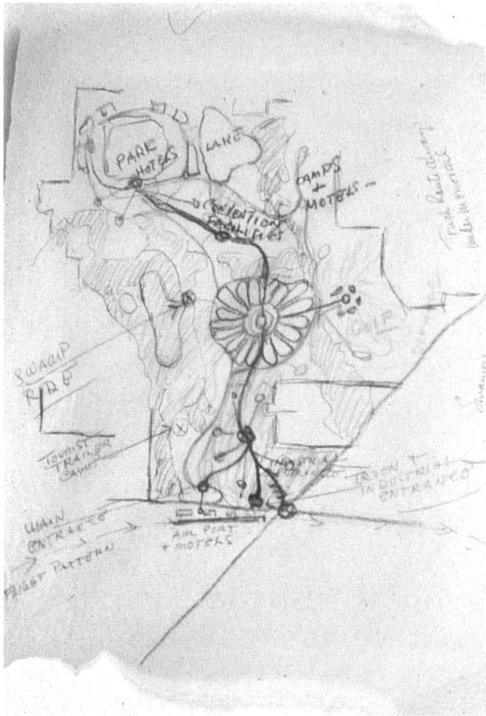


*The personal influence of Walt Disney on the Florida project cannot be overstated. At a 1966 meeting Walt showed this sketch, a footprint indicating spots for the theme park plus resort hotels, a lake, campgrounds, and more. Walt's drawing remained a basic model for Walt Disney World.*

## THE TORCH PASSES ON

In late 1966 Walt's health deteriorated rapidly, and he died in December of that year. The news shocked the world and stunned Walt's colleagues. But his creative heirs were prepared and eager to continue his work, including his Florida project. Walt himself had once said, "My greatest reward has been the ability to build this wonderful organization."

Leading the group was a man who had willingly spent most of his life in Walt Disney's formidable shadow. The two had fought others and fought one another. They had collaborated and conflicted, been both close and estranged. They had spent their entire lives combating and complementing one another. Now that Walt was gone, it was up to this other man to focus and guide Walt's successors and ensure the execution of his consummate dream. Walt's brother, Roy O. Disney, took up the Disney World project as his personal crusade.

It is impossible to separate the story of Walt Disney World from its creator, Walt Disney. Indeed, the Florida project was actually *re*named *Walt* Disney World by Roy. "Everybody knows the Ford car, but not everybody knows it was Henry Ford who started it all," Roy stated. "It's going to be *Walt* Disney World, so people will always know that this was Walt's dream."

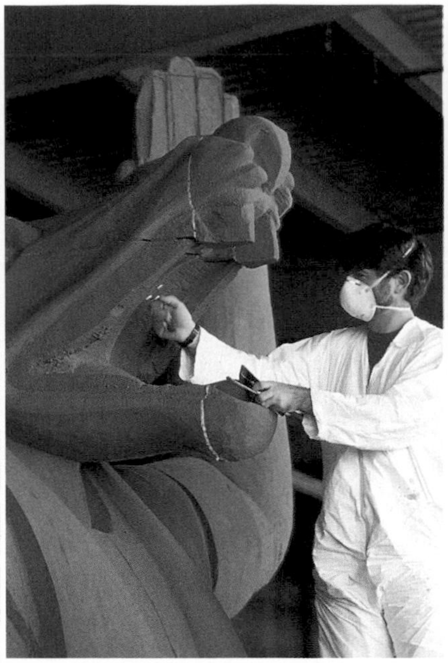

# CHAPTER TWO

# IMAGINEERING THE DREAM

Walt Disney and Roy O. Disney were archetypal siblings. Early in their lives they established a mutual bond of affection, protection, need, respect, and loyalty that lasted for their lives. Through their many ups and downs, Walt and Roy remained committed to one another's strengths. It is no understatement to say that Walt Disney World is the final symbol of the lifelong commitment between these two remarkable brothers.

From the time they formed Disney Brothers Studio in 1923 in Hollywood, Walt had dreamed the dreams and Roy had the often thankless task of figuring out how to turn wild dreams into sound business.

*Walt Disney (left) with his brother and business partner, Roy O. Disney, proudly celebrate their special Academy Award, won on November 18, 1932, "for the creation of Mickey Mouse."*

OPPOSITE:
*The many faces and phases of Walt Disney Imagineering in the process of creating Walt Disney World.*

## THE DISNEY BROTHERS

Over the years Roy and Walt had battled over nearly every major innovation that came along, from Technicolor in the 1930s to Disneyland in the 1950s. It wasn't that Roy lacked vision; it wasn't that he didn't support Walt's creative nature. Walt's creative vision just didn't time itself particularly well for the company's fiscal health. When Roy believed in a project—as he did with *Snow White and the Seven Dwarfs*, the new studio in Burbank, *20,000 Leagues Under the Sea,* and particularly Walt Disney World—he ran a close second to Walt in his enthusiasm for it.

Whether Roy ever received *public* recognition for his Herculean efforts on behalf of Walt Disney Productions, there was one significant acknowledgment of his expertise. Walt Disney knew Roy Disney's value. Walt knew that he and Roy were interdependent. "Roy and I must have a guardian angel," Walt told a reporter in the 1950s. "We could never split up like Dean Martin and Jerry Lewis. Roy doesn't know whether it's my guardian angel, and I don't know whether it's his." Walt knew that Roy was performing a vital function for the company, a function that Walt had neither interest nor expertise in but was crucial to their success.

*Before becoming a tourist attraction, Bay Lake was completely drained. The drained lake was then dredged of tons of silt, plant material, and debris. The bottom of the lake also yielded tons of white sand, which was relocated to create the beaches of Seven Seas Lagoon.*

At the Florida press conference in November 1965, Walt addressed the unique nature of the back-and-forth, give-and-take compromise that exemplified the way the Disney brothers did business: "My brother and I have been together in our business for 42 years now. He's my big brother. And he's the one that, when I was a little fella, I used to go to with some of my wild ideas, and he'd either straighten me out, put me on the right path or . . . if he didn't agree with me, I'd work on it for years until I got him to agree with me."

Eight years older than Walt, Roy attempted to retire at several points in the late 1950s and early 1960s. Walt opposed his departure at every turn, using threats, incentives, enticements, and the time-honored sibling techniques of guilt and obligation to keep Roy at work.

With Walt Disney's death in 1966, Roy's retirement plans were put on hold. The company couldn't take it. Roy's sense of obligation couldn't take it. And importantly, Roy truly believed that Disney World made sound business sense. At the age of 73, he hesitantly took charge of Walt Disney Productions. The Disney World project was his primary focus.

## BREAKING GROUND

Already, in September of 1965, William ("Joe") Potter had been brought in by the Disney brothers to supervise the Florida project, directly from his post as executive vice president of the 1964–65 New York World's Fair. Potter was a former major general in the Army Corps of Engineers and had served four years as governor of the Panama Canal Zone and as president of the Panama Canal Corporation.

In October 1965 the initial work began in Florida. Three hundred acres in the northwest corner of the property were cleared. Consulting engineers conducted water control and drainage studies on the site. Tree stump removal, leveling and grading of soil, and the planting of Pensacola Bahia grass and ryegrass were some of the initial activities on the Disney site. Gee & Jenson Consulting Engineers provided a detailed reclamation management proposal for the Reedy Creek Drainage District in August of 1966. This thorough plan included details of levees, canals, water control structures, bridges, culverts, roads, and other service facilities.

The initial planning for Walt Disney World began during a time when environmental issues were at the public forefront, and the impact of a development the size of the Florida project was put under heightened scrutiny because of the project's massive transformation of the character of the land. The commitment to balancing the needs of the project with the maintenance of the overall ecology and beauty of the property was established early in the project development. A 7,500-acre Walt Disney World Conservation Area was established in 1970 as a permanently managed and protected preserve of primitive acreage and virgin cypress trees.

The first task for the Reedy Creek Drainage District was to develop methods to drain areas of swampland for construction without damaging

the balance of the fragile water tables, and avoiding the ever-present danger of flooding. Since the whole of central Florida essentially floats on a body of freshwater, any depletion or damage to one part of this water supply could cause environmental imbalance and devastation to the entire region. After extensive planning, some 55 miles of canals and levees were constructed to control and exchange water levels without depleting the overall reserve. Water control structures keep the water levels in check by automatically floating open when the water level peaks and then automatically closing when those peaks subside. The gates require no monitoring, and they remove the risk of flooding or drought. Instead of following the invasive straight lines of most artificial canal systems, the intricate network of canals on Disney property is designed to follow the curves of the natural landscape, an idea originally conceived by Imagineer John Hench.

With the passage of a hefty legislation package in the spring of 1967, work on the Disney project began in earnest, on the site and in the headquarters of WED Enterprises (Disney's theme park design division) in Glendale, California.

## PHASE ONE

The Disney World undertaking was a massive one and put a strain on the fiscal and creative resources of Walt Disney Productions. For this reason, the

TOP:
*An early concept painting of Seven Seas Lagoon surrounded by (clockwise from top) the proposed Asian Hotel, Magic Kingdom, Contemporary Resort, Venetian Resort, and Polynesian Resort.*

BOTTOM:
*Instead of forming rigid straight lines, the Walt Disney World drainage canals were designed to appear natural.*

*Part of the extensive planning of the Magic Kingdom includes nine acres of underground utility corridors called utilidors, an urban basement providing out-of-sight access to infrastructural services. In addition to sewer lines, pipes, and cables, the utilidors house the premier United States use of the Swedish AVAC trash-disposal system, with trash funneled underground in pneumatic tubes to a central collection point. Also located here is the Digital Animation Control System (DACS), which ensures that the hundreds of Audio-Animatronics figures in the Magic Kingdom are "on cue" during their performances, by orchestrating more than 72,000 individual functions every second. DACS also opens theater doors, elevates stage lifts, operates lighting and curtains, and monitors fire protection, security, equipment failure, and power loss. The utilidors also provide a means of access for employees out of sight of park visitors.*

project was to be enacted in phases. Phase One called for the development of initial vacation destination amenities over a five-year period. The plan for the Phase One vacation kingdom, at the time of its announcement in 1968, included the Disneyland-like theme park, five resort hotels, an entrance complex, golf courses, and a variety of ancillary daytime resort activities. Site preparation started on May 30, 1967, with actual construction beginning in April 1969.

Once the property-wide water control and drainage infrastructure had been established, Imagineers in California began various projects simultaneously. Initially (and as has happened on many Disney projects since), Disney deferred to the acknowledged experts in this type of development and hired an outside group of engineers to oversee construction. The Disney staff wanted the resort built in two years. The consultant group, however, forecast that the project would take a minimum of five years. The Disney staff fired the consultants and created its own team. On-site construction became the purview of Admiral Joseph Fowler, who was president of WED Enterprises at the time.

SEVEN SEAS LAGOON

Extensive studies by air and on the ground had been conducted to determine the ideal locations for development. Bay Lake was the largest natural body of water (it was also one of the first areas of property that Walt had wanted to buy). It was felt that the acreage west of the lake was the ideal location for the theme park, and a large portion of the land was found to include areas of high ground, ideal for construction. At the same time, areas

## REEDY CREEK IMPROVEMENT DISTRICT

Developing 27,000 acres of Florida property into a destination resort required more than engineering and earth moving. The scale of Walt Disney World as a massive construction project was matched by Walt Disney World as a massive government relations and legislative project.

The scope of Walt Disney World has been described time and again as a land area approximately the size of the city of San Francisco, or twice the size of the island of Manhattan. This statistical metaphor immediately begs questions of regulation and enforcement of building and zoning codes, environmental and wildlife protection, taxation, and municipal government. Since the Walt Disney World property straddles the dividing line between Orange County on the north and Osceola County on the south, these issues were initially complicated by the jurisdiction of two county governing bodies.

The Reedy Creek Drainage District was formed in May 1966 through the General Drainage Act of Florida and by agreement of Orange and Osceola counties and the Florida Flood Control District. The district included all the Disney acreage, plus several smaller non-Disney tracts of privately owned land, and was enacted by ruling of the Florida Circuit Court.

Further Disney legislative proposals relating to the property and projects were sponsored by delegations from Orange and Osceola counties, who submitted them to the Florida state legislature in spring 1967. The legislation was divided into three acts. The first two nearly identical acts created two municipalities: one encompassing the northern portion of the Disney property including Bay Lake, known as the City of Bay Lake; the other encompassing the Disney property for a distance of about two miles on both sides of State Road 530, known as the City of Reedy Creek (now the City of Lake Buena Vista).

The third act created the Reedy Creek Improvement District, which encompasses the entire Disney property, and it assumed the functions of the Reedy Creek Drainage District. The act was a composite of special assessment, improvement, and taxing districts already provided for under existing Florida laws and had the effect of combining the services those districts perform within a single district under a single governing body. The act clarified the role of the Reedy Creek Improvement District in performing the work of drainage, solid waste collection, and flood and pest control. It also amplified the district's authority to build and maintain roadways, utilities, and sewer systems; to provide and administer public transportation, police, fire protection, and airport and parking facilities; and to regulate land use and planning within the district limits. In addition it covered the incidental powers necessary to implement and carry out the general purposes of the district. The largest section of the act dealt with the district's authority to issue bonds to finance any improvements necessary for the performance of the authorized services.

The act also set up a five-person board of supervisors, the governing body of the district. The board is responsible for all policy decisions by the district and authorizes all contracts, agreements, and construction projects to be performed by the district. It also adopts the budget; establishes utility and user fees, adopts building codes, land use regulations, and environmental regulations; and provides direction to the district administrator for the efficient operation of the district.

There was some initial fear that the legislation requested by Disney was so sweeping that Disney sovereignty would be subordinate only to that of the state of Florida, but some minor objections and revisions to the legislation were worked out between the Orange County Commission and Walt Disney Productions. The legislation passed the Florida house of representatives and senate and was signed into law by Governor Claude Kirk, Jr., in a special ceremony on May 12, 1967.

The advantages to this legislation were twofold. Disney could operate with a large degree of autonomous self-sufficiency on the Florida project. A single governing body, instead of two or more, could oversee public services and regulate building methods, codes, new technologies, and materials in keeping with the continual cutting-edge nature of the project. Second, Florida taxpayers would not contribute to Disney construction—and likewise Disney would not have to rely on state agencies for approval of anything it built.

The political and governmental foundation for Walt Disney World enabled physical construction to begin.

## ROY OLIVER DISNEY

While the public justifiably recognized the artistic genius of Walt Disney, they were seldom acquainted with the genius of his brother, Roy O. Disney, who provided the business leadership for Walt Disney Productions from its inception in 1923.

Spanning nearly 50 years, Roy's work always complemented Walt's creations. They were associated virtually from the beginning of Walt's pioneering of the animated motion picture field, with Roy handling the often-thankless business end of operations, while Walt pursued the more publicly captivating creative side of things.

Roy Disney once said, "My job is to help Walt do the things he wants to do." For years it was one of the most successful alliances in the entertainment industry.

Born in Chicago, Illinois, on June 24, 1893, Roy was one of five children of Elias and Flora Call Disney. After attending grammar school in Chicago, Roy went to high school in Marceline, Missouri, after the family moved there in 1906.

Like many youngsters of his time, he got his first taste of business delivering newspapers, running both a morning and an evening route, but taking it easy on Sundays, when he made only the morning delivery.

For eight years after graduation from high school, Roy worked as a bank clerk with the First National Bank of Kansas City. When World War I broke out, he joined the navy and for two years served as a petty officer on a cargo ship plying the submarine-infested waters of the Atlantic.

The rigors of the sea affected his health, so after mustering out, he moved to Arizona and spent three years there recuperating.

In August 1923 Walt moved from Kansas City to Hollywood, where he felt there would be a greater market for his work. Roy was in California by this time, too, and offered his support, sympathy, and encouragement—as well as $250. They pooled their resources (Walt had only $40), borrowed an extra $500 from an uncle, and began production of short films.

Soon after his arrival in Hollywood, Roy sent for Edna Francis, the girl with whom he'd fallen in love when they met in Kansas City. The couple was married in Hollywood in April 1925. (Their one son, Roy Edward, was born in January 1930 and is now vice chairman of The Walt Disney Company.)

Roy O. Disney began his motion picture career using a camera that Walt had set up in a small store building behind a Hollywood real estate office. This became their first studio. Walt had received an order from a New York distributing company for a series of shorts, and while he worked feverishly supervising the creation of the drawings, Roy acted as cameraman and bookkeeper.

Throughout the following years, Roy assumed full responsibility for the distribution and monetary functions of the organization. In 1926 the Disneys saw their financial status reach a position that enabled them to build their own studio, on Hyperion Avenue in the Silver Lake neighborhood of Hollywood.

The success of *Snow White and the Seven Dwarfs* in 1937 placed the Disneys at the top of the animation field. To meet their further expansion needs, in January 1940 they completed a new studio in Burbank, which still serves as worldwide headquarters for The Walt Disney Company.

For the next 31 years, Roy continued to supervise the business dealings of Walt Disney Productions, as its financial success continued to soar. After assuming personal supervision of the planning and construction of Walt Disney World, he directed the resort to its successful opening in October 1971. Roy O. Disney died soon afterward, on December 20, 1971.

Though the creative vision of Walt Disney is unceasingly acclaimed, the exceptional business genius of his brother, Roy, is what enabled Walt's visions to become real, and brought the company to the position of strong and highly diversified success it has enjoyed for decades.

In the end, Roy considered it a highlight of his career to be able to personally dedicate Walt Disney World as "a tribute to the philosophy and life of Walter Elias Disney." Walt Disney World is indeed a tribute to the lifelong fellowship of these two brothers and to their loyalty and commitment to one another.

of low wetland directly adjacent to the high ground were discovered to be unstable and useless for construction, even with extensive fill. Typically, the Disney team turned this disadvantage into part of the show. They decided to excavate the low land and transform it into a man-made lagoon, extending the natural waterway of Bay Lake westward.

Walt Disney World visitors know this waterway as Seven Seas Lagoon, over which they pass by either monorail or watercraft to reach the Magic Kingdom. The plan was in keeping with Walt Disney's desire to remove visual intrusions and enact the lessons learned at Disneyland, creating a true sense of place for the new park. (Translated to the layout of Disneyland, the location of Seven Seas Lagoon would be the Disneyland parking lot.)

Bay Lake was drained with pumps, and a bottom layer of root structures, silt, debris, and other muck was dredged out. More than seven million cubic yards of earth were dug up from the lagoon and used to raise the Magic Kingdom site an average of 14 feet. On the site where the park was to stand, a network of warehouse-sized rooms, hallways, and office space was built, then backfilled with more of the reclaimed earth from the lagoon construction. Thus, the Magic Kingdom that guests see above-pavement is actually the second and third stories of the buildings. This process created a nine-acre underground system of tunnels, called utilidors, which form a unique support basement. The utilidors provide easy, behind-the-scenes access to utility systems, offices, and storage areas, as well as out-of-sight passage to employee work locations. (This was another legacy from Walt Disney, who was perturbed when he saw a Western sheriff in Disneyland's Tomorrowland because the only way for the sheriff to get from costuming to his workplace was in guests' view.)

Underneath the mire at the bottom of Bay Lake, engineers found thousands of tons of pure white sand. The sand was removed and cleaned, and now lines the four and a half miles of beach that surround the 172-acre lagoon and Bay Lake. The lake and the new Seven Seas Lagoon were then filled with water from the surrounding wetland and stocked with more than 70,000 fingerling bass.

A tree farm was established, and there landscape designers tended thousands of plants, trees, shrubs, and flowers. A variety of plant forms from Asia, Australia, the Pacific Islands, and Africa were adapted to the central Florida soil and climate (some required more than three years of acclimation). The original inventory of trees alone numbered more than 8,000. The tree farm also housed about 1,500 existing trees in transit—those that had been moved from areas destined for development. By October 1970 Disney reported that more than 60,000 plants and 800 different varieties of trees had been acquired, moved, acclimated, and transplanted into the various islands, lagoons, jungles, and other locales around the Walt Disney World property.

*When Disney came to Florida, one of its very first horticultural efforts was to establish a tree farm. This first tree farm was located in what later became the North Service Area, north of the Magic Kingdom site. When the Magic Kingdom opened, the tree farm was relocated to its present site in the nursery complex, 190 acres in the South Service Area, in the southwest corner of the property.*

## WED ENTERPRISES
## WALT DISNEY IMAGINEERING

Science fiction writer and futurist Ray Bradbury once defined it as "a true Renaissance organization . . . the only people I see who are successful at changing the world are right here—people with very special dreams." It has also been described at various times as an "idea factory," a "dreamer's workshop," and a laboratory for "urban visionaries." Walt Disney Imagineering (WDI) is the master planning, creative development, design, engineering, production, and project management subsidiary of The Walt Disney Company, responsible for the creation of the Disney theme parks and their expansion.

But WDI, like so many parts of the present-day Walt Disney Company, can trace its current charter directly back to Walt Disney himself. He once said, "There's really no secret about our approach. We keep moving forward—opening up new doors and doing new things—because we're curious. And curiosity keeps leading us down new paths. We're always exploring and experimenting. We call it 'Imagineering,' the blending of creative imagination and technical know-how."

Walt founded what is now known as Walt Disney Imagineering in 1952, because he realized that he wouldn't be able to create Disneyland within the boundaries of the studio system. He initially named his new company Walt Disney Incorporated. Roy, however, was concerned about the possible confusion between the publicly held Walt Disney Productions and Walt's privately owned Walt Disney Incorporated. Walt then argeed to change the name to WED Enterprises (an acronym for Walter Elias Disney). WED Enterprises ultimately became a wholly owned business unit of The Walt Disney Company. And eventually, in 1986, WED was renamed, becoming Walt Disney Imagineering.

The Imagineering team today includes show designers, artists, writers, project managers, engineers, architects, filmmakers, audio and visual specialists, animators, manufacturing groups, computer programmers, land planners, ride system designers, finance experts, and researchers. Together, they are responsible for all phases of project development, from concept initiation to field art direction and show installation. WDI now maintains facilities in Glendale, California, and Long Island, New York, as well as on site at Disneyland, Walt Disney World, Tokyo Disneyland, and Disneyland Paris.

Many wonders of entertainment technology developed by WDI were initially seen in the Disney parks, including the United States' first daily operating monorail system (1959), a realistic adventure created by Audio-Animatronics characters (Pirates of the Caribbean, 1967), the first computer-controlled thrill ride (Space Mountain, 1975), an advanced 3-D motion picture photography system (*Magic Journeys*, 1982), along with a litany of other innovations.

Michael Eisner, chairman and chief executive officer of The Walt Disney Company, described his feelings about the unique dream plant behind all the wonders: "Walt Disney dreamed of a place where families could go to have fun together—a place of fantasy and magic. Disneyland was the first of many such places and Imagineering is where the real magic is created. I believe it is the most magical organization in the world."

## BEHIND (AND BELOW) THE SCENES

Walt's concept of the Florida project as the pinnacle of prototype implementation moved aggressively forward. The Disney team designed and built energy plants, maintenance shops, a food center, and a laundry to handle the massive needs of guests and employees. Miles of sewage, water, and electrical lines, pipes, and conduits were laid, paving the way for future utility plants. A waste-water treatment plant was built to treat effluent and direct treated waste water to the nearby tree farm and to golf courses for irrigation use.

The advanced central energy plant was completely integrated with the requirements of the overall property. The waste heat created by the turbine generators was captured for use in producing high-temperature hot water, chilled water, and compressed air. The high-temperature hot water, in turn, fulfilled demands for space heating, domestic hot water, cooking, and absorption chilling for air conditioning. An advanced computer system was installed in the central energy plant to monitor and control the distribution of power across the property. The system is designed to immediately recognize any problem occurring in the parks or hotels and to adjust the problem instantly and automatically from its remote location. The plant also produces a portion of the overall power requirement for the entire property, and in the case of a power outage (especially likely in thunderstorm-prone central Florida) it can provide emergency power.

The need to continually observe and monitor the delicate balance of the entire property's ecology was aided through the design and implementation of a comprehensive monitoring system, which detects smoke, fire, floods, or unusual water flow through sensory apparatus located in more than 3,000 sites across the property.

The property had no telephone lines or other telecommunication infrastructure. Walt Disney Productions formed a partnership with the Florida Telephone Company to create a new, state-of-the-art telephone system for Walt Disney World. Vista-United Telecommunications was initially designed to implement resort, park, and administration telephone service, as well as transmit computer data and video on the property. It became the first all-electronic telephone system using underground cable instead of overhead wires, as well as the first to use fiber optics in a commercial venture, and was the first telephone company in Florida to implement a 911 emergency system.

The mammoth needs of operating the resort on a day-to-day basis had to be addressed. If the sewer lines and electrical conduit constitute the resort hardware, the separate support infrastructure provided at Central Shops is the software. Built north of the Magic Kingdom, Central Shops serves as a major center for fabrication of just about everything, from trash cans and ride vehicles to signs and ornamental iron and wood work. The shops are divided into specialized areas, including the machine shop, metal shop, maintenance services, electrical, plumbing and air conditioning, staff

*All of the Walt Disney World employees are "themed," just as the buildings and attractions are, through the use of costumes and uniforms. The world's largest working wardrobe department creates and maintains costumes for employees—real and mechanical (including the Audio-Animatronics figures).*

OPPOSITE:
*At the Innoventions attraction in Epcot, "Alec Tronic" entertains and exhibits the latest Audio-Animatronics engineering.*

shop (where sculptural and molded elements are fabricated in a variety of materials), mill shop (woodworking and lumber), and paint shop. A dry dock was even built next to Central Shops for fabrication and servicing of watercraft.

Similarly, since there was no food distribution center in central Florida large enough to support the volume of resort and theme park guests, Disney had to build its own. All food was shipped to a central plant before distribution to various locations on the property. The center had its own bakery and a kitchen for preparing soups and sauces, meat, pizza, sandwiches, and salads. There was also a quality-control kitchen, to monitor and keep recipes consistent property-wide and to evaluate menu items being prepared in the central kitchen.

In addition to themed buildings and attractions, all of Walt Disney World's employees needed to be themed, through the use of costumes and uniforms. The world's largest working wardrobe department, with facilities in the Magic Kingdom and each of the hotels, was assigned to create and maintain costumes for employees—real and mechanical (the clothes of the Audio-Animatronics figures fall under the supervision of the wardrobe department, too). The largest laundry facility in the world was also created, not only for these costumes, but for the more than 100,000 pounds of linens handled each day by employees and visitors.

The original resort hotels used a prototype unitized construction method known as modular construction. WED Enterprises and the Los

# AUDIO-ANIMATRONICS®

During the late 1940s and early 1950s, Walt Disney's penchant for high-tech tinkering led to one of the oddest sideline projects of his career. Called "Project Little Man," it was actually a first pass at what would come to be regarded as robotics. It involved the animation of a small-scale human figure in a miniature proscenium vaudeville stage, operated by cables and crude, hand-cut cam discs. And it worked. Walt quickly set the team to work on a miniature Barbershop Quartet, with a still-ambiguous concept of how these little shows might be exhibited.

A few years after Disneyland opened, the burgeoning electronics industry provided the means for Walt Disney to realize his dream of dimensional animation. His idea was that in Disneyland guests would be seated in a Chinese restaurant, and in the center of the room the great Chinese philosopher Confucius would sit, conveying ancient insight and wisdom to his dinner guests. Confucius would not be an actor, though—he would be a full-scale human robot. Research began with animation of a life-size head. Walt's mechanical wizards, Roger Broggie and Wathel Rogers, developed a solenoid coil, a cylindrical coil of wire that created a magnetic field, to activate the controls. They even experimented with new advances in latex technology for the realistic "skin" that covered the head. It worked. It simply didn't work well enough for public exhibition—yet.

Another project supplanted the Confucius head research. Work began on dozens of parrots, cockatoos, macaws, and toucans for a revue by enchanted birds. A new technology replaced the cumbersome cable and cam and solenoid coil method. With this technique, a 14-channel tape carried show voices and music as well as audio tones to cue the mechanical, electrical, and hydraulic actions. Audio-Animatronics was born.

Walt Disney's Enchanted Tiki Room premiered at Disneyland to an enthusiastic response in June 1963. The show still plays at Disneyland, Walt Disney World, and Tokyo Disneyland. (Another Audio-Animatronics bird had a cameo appearance in Walt Disney's 1964 film classic *Mary Poppins*. In "Spoonful of Sugar," Julie Andrews shares a whistling duet with an Audio-Animatronics robin.)

Walt Disney's work on the 1964–65 New York World's Fair included the crowning exhibition of his new robotic technology, the Lincoln figure created for Great Moments with Mr. Lincoln. It was the almost coercive development of this show under a strict deadline that pushed the evolution of Audio-Animatronics to a point where its technology was usable on a daily basis.

Nearly every Disney theme park attraction since has featured at least a component of Audio-Animatronics, including Pirates of the Caribbean, The Haunted Mansion, The Hall of Presidents, Country Bear Jamboree, America Sings, Jim Henson's Muppet™ Vision 3D, Star Tours, and The ExtraTERRORestrial Alien Encounter.

In the 1980s Disney set up a collaborative research project with the University of Utah medical prosthetic laboratory, sharing data that led Disney to more highly developed natural animation and the university to better prosthetic technology. This work resulted in the Audio-Animatronics "compliance system," which more accurately replicates the natural give-and-take of the human musculature. Figures made with the new technology were dubbed "A–100" figures. This motion technology is well displayed in the Wicked Witch of the West in The Great Movie Ride (Disney-MGM Studios), Alec Tronic at Innoventions (Epcot), and the figure in the preshow of The ExtraTERRORestrial Alien Encounter (Magic Kingdom).

## AROUND THE WORLD IN 14.7 LANE MILES: THE MONORAIL SYSTEM

The concept of mass transit via elevated vehicles certainly isn't new. Even the idea of those vehicles carried on or suspended from a single beam—the monorail—isn't new. Research on the principle occurred even before the invention of the airplane or automobile. As early as 1878 a steam-powered monorail system operated between the towns of Bradford and Gilmore, California. In 1892 an electric car running on a single rail operated on Long Island in New York. History's longest continuously operating monorail, the Schwebebahn in Wuppertal, Germany, has been running since 1901.

In 1958 Disney and Alweg Company of Cologne, Germany, collaborated to develop a working prototype for daily use at Disneyland. The Disneyland Monorail System opened in 1959 with two trains and a track running for eight-tenths of a mile. The trains straddled a concrete beam with rubber-tire drive and braking wheels on top of the beamway; guiding and stabilizing wheels contacted with the sides of the beam. Each Disneyland train was powered by four 100-horsepower, 600-volt direct current motors and got its electrical power from a metallic busbar located alongside the beam. In 1969 WED designed and manufactured a new fleet of four five-car trains to replace the decade-old originals. The new cars, called Mark III, had greater passenger capacity, operated more efficiently, and required less maintenance.

Mass transit—and monorail trains—were part of the Walt Disney World project from its conception. The Florida monorail beamway was made of concrete with a special polystyrene core to lighten its weight; it came by standard dual-rail train from Tacoma, Washington. The monorail trains themselves, dubbed Mark IV, were constructed by WED in California. Initial plans called for monorail tracks to circle Seven Seas Lagoon, one going straight to the Magic Kingdom from the main parking lot, the other stopping at the resort hotels around Seven Seas Lagoon. Future plans called for the beam to extend to Lake Buena Vista, where the Disney Village Resort was under development. (This extended route never made it past the planning stages.)

The original monorail track ran in a loop directly through the concourse of the Contemporary Resort, to the Polynesian Resort, the Magic Kingdom gate, and the Ticket and Transportation Center. In 1982 the monorail was extended with a four-mile run to EPCOT Center, including a scenic loop through Future World. Today there are 14.7 miles of rail, including all spurlines.

In December 1989 the Walt Disney World Monorail System was refitted with 12 all-new Mark VI trains (the Mark V model had debuted in Disneyland in April 1987). These six-car trains include taller cars with redesigned interiors and expanded standing room, increasing overall system capacity by 30 percent. The 200-foot-long trains are constructed of high-strength composite honeycomb material, which reduces overall train weight without sacrificing structural strength.

The Walt Disney World Monorail System carries an average weekday ridership of 150,000 passengers—more than 50,000,000 riders per year. Since the opening of Walt Disney World in 1971, the system has carried more than a billion passengers. In 1986 the Disney Monorail System was declared a National Historic Mechanical Engineering Landmark by the American Society of Mechanical Engineers.

Angeles architectural firm Welton Becket and Associates designed the Contemporary Resort and Polynesian Resort hotels in partnership with United States Steel. While the hotels' skeletal structures were being erected, their rooms were manufactured separately at an assembly plant three miles away. Each was built as a lightweight (about six-ton) steel module, completely outfitted with wall coverings, air-conditioning equipment, bathroom fixtures, mirrors, and doors. The finished rooms were trucked to the site and then individually lifted by crane and slid into the hotel's framework, as if it were a gigantic chest of drawers.

Transportation systems were also constructed throughout the property. Monorail trains were manufactured in Orlando by Martin-Marietta. The old-fashioned steam locomotives that circle the park were found in Mexico and refurbished in Tampa. A 150-vessel armada was assembled in St. Petersburg, including paddle-wheel steamboats, ferryboats, jungle launches, canoes, keelboats, and submarines.

### BEHIND (AND ABOVE) THE SCENES

Back in Glendale, the Imagineers at WED Enterprises were equally hard at work designing the themed environments, structures, attractions, entertainment, and shows that would comprise the Magic Kingdom and, to a lesser extent, the resort hotels. The Imagineers supervised the creation of the Magic Kingdom from the tiniest mosaic tile to the show and ride systems of the park's 23 opening-day attractions.

Aboveground construction of the Magic Kingdom began in late 1969, starting with Main Street, U.S.A. and Cinderella Castle. Years of research went into the planning and design of this distinctive signature building. Disney legend Herbert Ryman began with a charcoal sketch, a design he developed further in a famous and often-published painting. He used several French castles for his inspiration, among them Chambord, Ussé, and Chenonceau. Inspiration also came from the classic Walt Disney animated feature *Cinderella.*

Since no one had built a 189-foot-high castle in America, it was difficult to find experienced craftspeople, so WED artists and engineers took on much of the job, which took 18 months to complete. Six hundred tons of steel were used in the framework. Imagineers then sculpted exterior and interior walls to resemble solid granite. The 10 towering spires, fabricated and finished in an old fertilizer factory about five miles away, were slid into place above the main building and permanently attached (contrary to myth, the castle cannot be, nor has it ever been, dismantled in the event of a hurricane). Space for an apartment for the Disney family was designed and built inside the castle's upper floors, but it has never been completed or used. Finishing touches applied to this architectural marvel included Cinderella's mice friends carved into decorative columns and the Disney family crest in stone above the breezeways.

During the countdown period, the project also had the benefit of a chief expediter, in the person of Dick Nunis. Nunis had been at Disneyland since 1955 and was an executive in operations there from 1961. He regularly commuted to Orlando beginning in 1967, as chairman of the Walt Disney World Operating Committee. As opening day drew near, Nunis was asked by corporate management if the October 1 opening date was achievable. When Nunis flatly answered "no," they authorized him to throw every resource of the company toward meeting the opening date. Back in the Glendale office, Richard ("Dick") Irvine, vice president and director of design for WED Enterprises; Joe Fowler, a former navy admiral who helped build Disneyland; and William ("Joe") Potter, who had been involved with the Florida project since 1965, were heading the team of Imagineers designing the park.

THE HUMAN TOUCH

The last component for the Florida project was perhaps the most important. Interviewing for the 6,200 employees required to operate the park, hotels, resort amenities, and support services began in earnest in June 1971. By March of that year, Disney recruiters had already received 30,000 to 40,000 job inquiries. Some 1,800 prospective employees were walking into the employment center each week, and another 8,000 applications arrived each month by mail. Florida residents were given first consideration. By the time

*Before construction* (ABOVE) *even began, years of research went into the design of Cinderella Castle. Herbert Ryman sketched the design of the structure* (LEFT), *and he later elaborated this vision in a famous painting* (OPPOSITE).

*Critics have tried to find something terribly funny—or sinister—in the extensive training programs for Walt Disney World employees. Perhaps the best capsule explanation of why Disney spends so much effort in employee education comes directly from a Walt Disney World employee handbook.*

*"Imagine yourself as a guest, bringing your family to visit Walt Disney World. You walk down Main Street, pass through Cinderella Castle, and suddenly come upon a Disney character sitting at a table, chatting with a supervisor over a cup of coffee and a cigarette. Doesn't sound like Disney, does it? And if you were that guest, you wouldn't be very happy with our show, would you? Remember that regardless of where you work or what your role is, anytime you are in a public area, you are 'onstage.' Your attitude and performance are direct reflections on the quality of our Walt Disney World show."*

the 1971 Walt Disney Productions annual report was released in January of 1972, the Walt Disney World employee base was assessed at more than 8,000 people. It was reported that only one in a dozen applicants was finally hired. Mandatory enrollment in The Disney University began orientation and training in the Disney way of doing things, the first step to earning the designation "Cast Member."

OPENING DAZE

The Walt Disney World Preview Center opened nearby in Lake Buena Vista in June 1970. In this attractive temporary building, visitors could see a large model and view paintings, drawings, and demonstrations about the forthcoming vacation kingdom. Prior to the opening of the resort in October 1971, more than one million visitors had a sneak preview of Walt Disney World from a staff of tour guides using artists' renderings, models, slides, and a motion picture. Also, from Labor Day through September 30, employees and their families, construction workers, civic leaders, and local businesspeople were admitted to the Magic Kingdom for "test runs."

Opening day on October 1 would lead to an entire preview month, with an opening gala and a 90-minute NBC-TV special scheduled for October 25. Media estimates of opening-day crowds anticipated that as many as 100,000 people would attend. Extra Florida state troopers were brought in to deal with the anticipated traffic snarls. October 1 proved anticlimactic. Apparently the alarming media estimates and the extension of opening celebrations over the entire month had done what they were intended to do—

only 10,000 visitors came through the gates of the Magic Kingdom on the first day of operations.

Although the pundits were quick to proclaim the failure of Disney's new venture, Disney veterans smiled and remembered similar criticism on the opening day of Disneyland 16 years before. The operation had run smoothly, no major operational problems had occurred, and the new staff had a busy but measured opportunity to gain their sea legs on the month-long shakedown cruise. (The crowds grew, slowly and steadily, over the following weeks. Barely one month later, on Thanksgiving Day 1971, cars were backed up onto the four-lane Interstate 4 highway for miles in what many locals recall as one of the worst traffic jams in the history of central Florida.)

It had been the largest privately funded construction project in the world. More than 9,000 workers labored in its construction. It cost $400 million to get to opening day. Throughout the entire process of development, engineering, and construction Roy O. Disney continued to guide and supervise his brother's last, great vision. On October 25, 1971, Roy stood alongside Mickey Mouse in the Town Square of the Magic Kingdom before an assembled crowd of celebrities, dignitaries, employees, and family and paid his final tribute to his celebrated brother and their lifelong collaboration:

> *Walt Disney World is a tribute to the philosophy and life of Walter Elias Disney . . . and to the talents, the dedication, and the loyalty of the entire Disney organization that made Walt Disney's dream come true. May Walt Disney World bring Joy and Inspiration and New Knowledge to all who come to this happy place . . . a Magic Kingdom where the young at heart of all ages can laugh, and play, and learn . . . together.*

*Roy O. Disney at the dedication ceremony of the Magic Kingdom, on October 25, 1971. After the death of his brother, Walt, in December 1966, Roy had dedicated his life to seeing through Walt's last great dream. Roy himself died less than two months after this photograph was taken, on December 20, 1971.*

# CHAPTER THREE

# THE MAGIC KINGDOM

*I've always said there will never be another Disneyland, and I think it's going to work out that way. This concept here will have to be something that is unique, so there is a distinction between Disneyland in California and whatever Disney does in Florida.*

—WALT DISNEY

OPPOSITE:
*Inspiration for the magical Cinderella Castle—the entrance to Fantasyland—came from Disney's animated feature of the fairy tale as well as actual French châteaux, including those of Chambord, Ussé, and Chenonceau.*

The centerpiece of the Phase One development of Walt Disney World was the Magic Kingdom, a theme park of similar design to California's Disneyland. This park provided much of the visual interest for the media covering the resort's opening and continued to be its primary entity for the next 10 years. A common misconception of those uninitiated to Walt Disney World is that it is just a theme park, "another Disneyland" in Florida. It's a twofold misinterpretation: first, Walt Disney World is a complete resort, with hotels, recreation, and other amenities, and second, the Magic Kingdom is not just a knockoff of Disneyland.

Certainly the Magic Kingdom intentionally follows the unique design of Disneyland, but far from being a cookie-cutter park, the Magic Kingdom expands upon the operational and aesthetic knowledge gained in more than a decade of Disneyland operation.

## LEARNING FROM EXPERIENCE

The basic layout of Disneyland, the hub-and-spoke design, was unique among parks, fairs, and museums. In his many research excursions prior to the building of Disneyland, Walt Disney noted several things that bothered him about such enterprises. The disharmony of architecture, different businesses fighting for visual attention, and plain ugliness or uncleanliness were

primary annoyances to Walt. He saw that the meandering layout of many of these enterprises disoriented visitors, causing them to get lost, and led to what Walt called "museum feet"—the ache of having walked too much just to get *through* the place.

Walt solved these problems by laying out Disneyland as an inverted triangle, with guests entering at the lowest point of the triangle and being led to its center by a corridor, Main Street, U.S.A. From the southern end of Main Street, guests always had a central point of reference, the "hub" and the castle, to help orient them through their journey. An earthen berm around the whole exterior of the park removed intrusive external views and eliminated the natural horizon line—allowing Disney Imagineers to create their own.

These lessons, combined with the basic storytelling elements of Disneyland, were certainly the *beginning* of the Magic Kingdom, but there is little actual duplication. "The blessing of size," as Walt called it, enabled Disney Imagineers to enlarge the scale and increase the operational efficiency of their new park, and expand the overall grandeur of the design approach. The spires of Cinderella Castle, for instance, soar to a full 189 feet, more than 100 feet taller than the intimate Sleeping Beauty Castle in Disneyland. While Sleeping Beauty Castle is seen by guests only once they are inside the park, it is critical that Cinderella Castle be seen from afar. Visitors, who have to make a six-mile drive after leaving the main highway in order to reach the Magic Kingdom, need to be reassured that the theme park is actually there. Additionally, it is important for the castle to be seen from the hotels, the monorail, and the ferry.

OPPOSITE:
*The Magic Kingdom from the air, looking north from the Main Street Station toward Cinderella Castle.*

*Cinderella Castle takes on many moods at different times of the day and from different points of view. Dick Irvine, vice president and director of design for WED; Bill Martin, a WED vice president in charge of the master layout of the Magic Kingdom; and Herbert Ryman, art director, were responsible for the magical look of the castle.*

# DISNEYLAND

In a 1948 memo Walt Disney described an idea for a "Mickey Mouse Park" to be built on a vacant 16-acre parcel of land across Riverside Drive, south of the Disney Studio. The park would include a turn-of-the-century town square, a Main Street, a Western street, and a miniature railroad. Walt set animator Ken Anderson to work in a special project room at the Disney Studio (to which only they had keys), developing concept sketches for his "Mickey Mouse Park." (Harper Goff did all the site plans.)

One of Walt's hobbies was miniature-making. He also loved trains. Combining the two, and inspired by animators and fellow train buffs Ollie Johnston and Ward Kimball, Walt constructed his own backyard rail system, which he called the Carolwood Pacific (Walt's home was on Carolwood Drive in the Holmby Hills neighborhood of Los Angeles). The locomotive, which Walt named the "Lilly Belle" after his wife, Lillian, was built with the assistance of Roger Broggie in the studio machine shop. Walt wrote to a friend, "My hobby, which also includes a miniature train, is a lifesaver. When I work with these small objects, I become so absorbed that the cares of the studio fade away . . . at least for a time."

The idea for a park continued to percolate in Walt's mind. While he happily hosted rides on the Carolwood Pacific, he tried to think of ways to combine and present to the public the trains, the miniatures, the nostalgic buildings, and the "Mickey Mouse Park" in a manner that was consistent with the Disney brand of entertainment and showmanship.

Walt's dream park idea grew too large for the acreage adjacent to the Disney Studio, so he commissioned studies from Stanford Research Institute to find an ideal location. In 1954 construction began in the midst of orange and walnut groves in the sleepy hamlet of Anaheim, about 30 miles south of Los Angeles. The imagined "Mickey Mouse Park" was becoming the real Disneyland.

After enormous financial stress and great personal risk to his reputation, Walt Disney realized a new era of success with Disneyland. And, in the process, he completely redefined the amusement park and added new words to the lexicon of entertainment.

But this success, as was always the case with Walt Disney, led him on to his next challenge. The land surrounding Disneyland, which had been out of Walt's fiscal reach, had been snapped up and immediately blighted with motels, restaurants, and other tacky symbols of the American car culture. Walt often said that he was ashamed to have caused Disneyland's perimeter to become a "second-rate Las Vegas," and he wondered about solutions to the urban blight he saw on Harbor Boulevard. What if he could control not only the arrival point, but, also the entire surrounding area? What if he could tell his story all the way from the guests' approach to the end of their visit? The seeds of Walt Disney World were planted in Anaheim.

In the first promotional announcements for the Magic Kingdom, there was a concerted effort to publicize the differences between (and ignore the similarities of) the new park and the already-established Disneyland. Thus, early publicity focused on projected plans for attractions that would premiere in Florida: Country Bear Jamboree, Liberty Square, The Hall of Presidents, Space Mountain, 20,000 Leagues Under the Sea, and Mickey Mouse Revue.

*Although most park visitors are unaware of the connection, the Walt Disney World steam trains make a personal statement about Walt Disney, who was fascinated with railroading. The narrow-gauge steam-powered locomotives were originally built in 1915 to 1928 but were completely revamped for the Magic Kingdom.*

## THE LAYOUT OF THE MAGIC KINGDOM

Encircling the Magic Kingdom is the Walt Disney World Railroad, a mile and a half of scenic railway meant to lend character and story to the foot of the Victorian Main Street, to draw a boundary around the community of the Magic Kingdom, and to give visitors a means to travel to the various "lands" of the Magic Kingdom—as well as a chance to get their bearings by taking a circuit tour of the entire kingdom. The trains are also a personal statement about Walt Disney and his fascination with railroading. The steam engines are named "Walter E. Disney," "Roy O. Disney," "Lilly Belle" (after Walt's wife, Lillian Bounds Disney), and "Roger E. Broggie" (the Disney Studios machinery wizard who helped Walt start his model railroading hobby and was the head of MAPO, the prototype manufacturing and production division of WED). The narrow-gauge steam-powered locomotives were built in the United States by the Baldwin Locomotive Company between 1915 and 1928, and when Disney scouts found the engines, they were hauling jute, sugar, hemp, and passengers for the United Railways of Yucatan in Mexico. They were dismantled and shipped to Tampa, where they were completely renovated and rebuilt for their Disney duty, with their wood-burning steam engines converted to high-grade, clean-burning diesel-fuel burners. Each locomotive now pulls five open-sided scenic passenger cars.

The entry to the Magic Kingdom is through tunnels beneath the Main Street Railroad Station, a grand terminal evoking the bustling early days of American passenger rail travel. Emerging from the tunnels, visitors find themselves in the grand Town Square, looking north down a filigreed Victorian city street toward an 18-story fairy-tale castle in the distance.

*A tribute to the design magic of Disney Imagineers, the view down a gingerbread Victorian city street toward an 18-story fairy-tale castle seems as natural as if the castle were a magnificent town library or civic hall.*

## MAIN STREET, U.S.A.

Main Street, U.S.A. is actually constructed as four individual buildings, or "blocks" (Northwest, Northeast, Southwest, and Southeast), bisected in the center by a crossroads (Center Street, appropriately). Each of these four main buildings is cleverly designed to appear as a grouping of individual and distinctive structures. Inside, each shop or attraction is treated with different decor, ornament, and materials as appropriate to the function and story being told. Disney Imagineers are ever vigilant in avoiding visual contradictions and intrusions that might interfere with the basic storytelling in each project.

At the south end of Main Street is Town Square, the civic center, with the Main Street Railroad Station, City Hall, and a municipal park, complete with flagpole. At the north end of Main Street is the Plaza, known colloquial-

EMPORIUM
TEDDY BEARS

*Looking down Main Street toward Cinderella Castle.*

OPPOSITE:
*Clockwise from top left: Past visions of the future in Tomorrowland, the brooding gothic facade of The Haunted Mansion, the Fife and Drum Corps in Liberty Square, the arid American Southwest of Big Thunder Mountain Railroad, gloomy crooner Big Al from the Country Bear Jamboree, exotic icons of Adventureland, the Victorian splendor of the glittering Crystal Palace, fond memories of a century past on Main Street, the denizens of Duckburg in Mickey's Starland, Disney storybook dreams come to life in Fantasyland. In the center: Cinderella Castle shows another beautiful countenance at dusk.*

ly as "the hub." It is from this point that most of the other realms of the Magic Kingdom may be entered.

Main Street lives up to its description as "the crossroads of an era: The gas lamp giving way to the electric light, the sputtering 'horseless carriage' challenging Old Dobbin for the streetcar right-of-way." Throughout the day it is alive with vehicles. A quaint horse-drawn streetcar plods along its leisurely rail-track route from north to south and back again, while more modern, motorized jitneys (with special mufflers to create the appropriate sputtering sound) and even a fire engine add to the bustle.

Storefront businesses appropriate to this nostalgic atmosphere abound on Main Street—a bakery, ice cream parlor, candy shop, jewelry boutique, and magic shop among them. An old-time barber shop and a wood-planked general store with its potbellied stove add to the street's turn-of-the-century ambiance. Above, the second-story "offices" carry window advertisements bearing the names of Disney executives, contributing artists, and family. Roy E. Disney and his wife, Patty, are featured, as are Dick Nunis, chairman of Walt Disney Attractions; John Hench, Disney artist since 1939 (later executive vice president of WED); WED design head Dick Irvine; Bill Martin, a WED vice president; Donn B. Tatum, former chairman of the board of Walt Disney Productions, CEO, and chairman of the executive committee; and E. Cardon ("Card") Walker, former Walt Disney Productions CEO.

Main Street Cinema pays homage to the early motion picture industry that gave Walt Disney his start. The tiny movie house initially showed a variety of silent films on a semicircular array of six screens. In 1978 the show was changed to a selection of Mickey Mouse cartoons. Finally, in December 1994, the Main Street Cinema began showing the world premiere screenings of *Mickey's Big Break*, a fanciful history of Mickey Mouse's 1928 "audition" for Walt, followed by a Mickey Mouse short cartoon. (*Mickey's Big Break* was created as a prologue for a screen-test attraction at Disney-MGM Studios but never used. Walt's nephew, Roy E. Disney, appears as his legendary uncle.)

# THE GARDENS: LANDSCAPING AND HORTICULTURE

From the earliest designs for Disneyland, the creative use of trees, flowers, and other plants has been as integral to the overall design and appeal of Disney parks and resorts as themed architecture and cleanliness. The variety of landscaping in Walt Disney World ranges from the exotic jungles of Adventureland in the Magic Kingdom to the formality of The American Adventure Rose Garden at Epcot to the casual glamour of the palm-lined Hollywood Boulevard at Disney-MGM Studios. Well over a million trees, shrubs, and flowers are part of the entertainment at Walt Disney World; each plant is placed to add character, color, mood, or backdrop to one of the world's largest stages.

Since the 1971 opening of Walt Disney World, some 100,000 trees and more than one million tended shrubs have been planted. Gardeners also plant more than two million bedding plants annually, in 300,000-plus square feet of flower beds. In addition to benefiting from seasonal crop rotation, flower beds are inspected daily, and replacements are made to maintain the desired show quality. Topiary can be found in more than 100 different designs, ranging from trees pruned in geometric shapes to the many Disney character topiary figures that dot the landscape throughout Walt Disney World.

The trees used at Walt Disney World come from all over the United States, but many of their ancestors have roots in Europe, Mexico, or the Orient. In all, there are 1,700 species of plants, representing flora gathered from not just the United States. but also 50 foreign countries. More than 2,000 miles of irrigation pipe and 50,000 sprinkler heads help keep everything healthy and growing. A sophisticated computerized system controls and monitors irrigation throughout the three theme parks.

ABOVE:
*Topiary designs are a staple at Walt Disney World, and these intricately molded models of Mickey and Minnie are examples of the art at its finest.*

LEFT:
*An enormous Mickey Mouse face made entirely of flowers greets guests as they enter the Magic Kingdom. A team of horticulturists regularly transplants flowers to keep Mickey looking fresh and colorful.*

"Aita Peatea," the motto of Disney's Polynesian Resort, means: "There will be another day tomorrow just like today"—and Maui, the god of vacations, slows the sun down to make the days longer in this South Seas resort. The Great Ceremonial House serves as the hotel's landmark and main reception center. Its warm cedarwood exterior is topped by 37 outrigger beams on each side—a total of 74 crisscrossing beams peaking 42 feet above the roof. The atmosphere created at the Polynesian is one of warmth, welcome, and soothing tropical relaxation.

Inside, the Polynesian awes visitors with the tropical spectacle of the Great Ceremonial House. A central waterfall cascades off the crags of volcanic stone, and coconut palms tower over a horticulturist's dreamland of anthuriums, ferns, gardenias, banana plants, orchids, and other subtropical and tropical plants—there are 75 varieties of foliage plants.

The South Pacific theme continues throughout the resort with white sand beaches, luxurious landscaping, rushing waterfalls, themed pools and longhouses, torch-lit walkways, and colorful costumes. The large site and meandering layout of the Polynesian give it a distinct feeling of tropical otherworldliness, and many frequent Walt Disney World guests cite it as one of the resort's treasures.

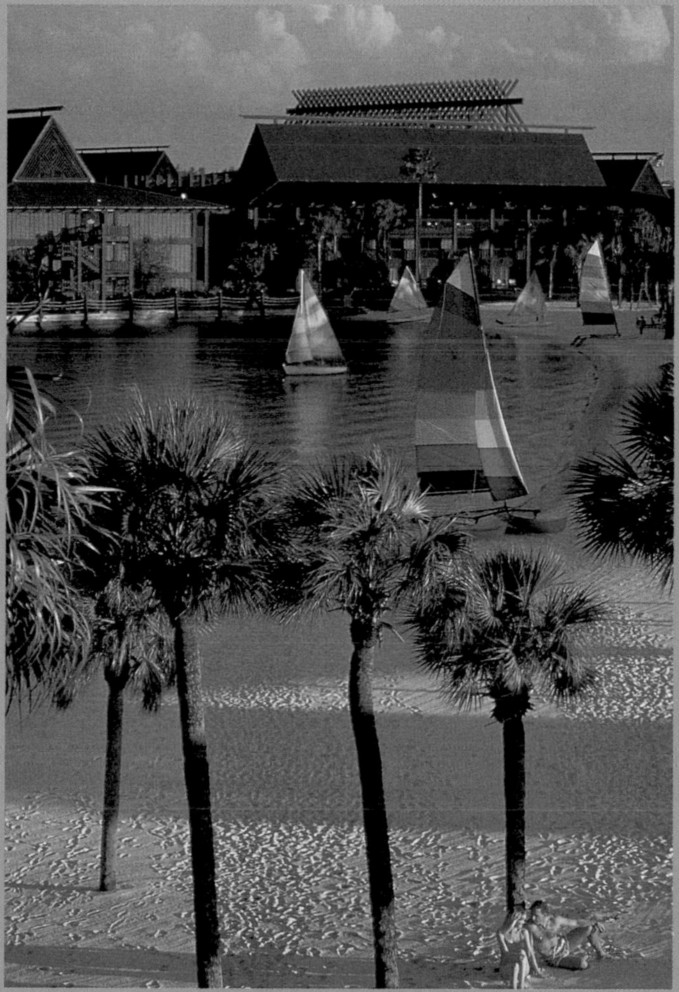

Disney's Polynesian Resort expanded in 1985, at which time all the guest rooms were upgraded. The 39-acre complex contains a number of buildings, including the Great Ceremonial House, a suite building, and several long houses named after various South Pacific islands, real (Tahiti, Samoa, Hawaii, Maui, and others) as well as fictional (Bali Hai). Within the resort there are five shops, three restaurants, a snack bar, two lounges, two swimming pools, and a game room.

The Polynesian Revue (also known as Kauai-Pono Polynesian Revue and Polynesian Luau) was originally held nightly at Seven Seas Lagoon, where guests sat on the white sand beaches and dined while viewing the show. As the luau grew in popularity, the Luau Cove was built to provide guests a more comfortable facility to enjoy the show without having to contend with sand in their shoes—or those occasional Florida showers.

*The Swiss Family Treehouse in three stages of "growth."* TOP: *Structural steel "limbs" reach skyward.* CENTER: *Scaffolding encloses the tree structure during the application of foliage.* BOTTOM: *The* Disneyodendron eximus *with its final growth.*

The Walt Disney Story opened in Town Square in 1973, the 50th anniversary of Walt Disney Productions. This fascinating historical exhibit featured an extensive display of Disney memorabilia, as well as a documentary film biography of Walt Disney, which was presented simultaneously in two 300-seat theaters. The attraction closed in October 1992, but its lobby and memorabilia display remain and are occasionally open.

As Main Street makes its way to the central Plaza, the theme park show dissolves into new scenes. Encircling the Plaza is a waterway, sloping green lawns, and lush landscape of flower beds and trees. (From 1973 to 1983 Victorian swan boats plied the short waterway around the Plaza.) On the southwest corner of the Plaza is the Crystal Palace, which houses a restaurant facility. From a design standpoint, the Crystal Palace acts as a visual transition between the urban Victorian Main Street and the tropical Adventureland entrance. The sunny glass-ceilinged atrium of the restaurant echoes not only the architectural styles of Main Street, but also the elegant hothouses, conservatories, and aviaries of the 19th-century period of British colonial rule.

## ADVENTURELAND

Adventureland is probably best described as movie exotica, since it combines so many foreign locales—Polynesia, Africa, the Caribbean, and Southeast Asia—into one romantic fantasy of exotic exploration. Much of the kinetic feel of Adventureland can be attributed to its complex landscaping: there is a veritable tangle of plant species throughout the area. Imagineer Morgan ("Bill") Evans was principally responsible for the design and development of the Walt Disney World landscaping "show."

Cape honeysuckle, Chinese hibiscus, Mexican flame vines, Brazilian bougainvillea, sword ferns, spider plants, and Australian tree ferns all thrive in Adventureland. This in itself was something of a feat for the Disney horticulturists, since the Adventureland region of the Magic Kingdom construction site was part of an extensive clay landfill, executed to raise and level the overall grade of the site. Buildings and facilities benefited from the solid ground underfoot, but when landscape designers arrived, they found a solid 14-inch bed of impervious clay in many landscape areas. To enable trees to survive, generous pits were dug to contain their root structure, and borings were made through the clay to the natural grade. The holes were filled with a sand and soil mix to allow vertical drainage and natural root development.

One gigantic plant that had no trouble taking root in the inhospitable clay landfill was the rare *Disneyodendron eximus*, the "hardwood" home of the Swiss Family Treehouse. Based on the 1960 Disney feature *Swiss Family Robinson*, which was based on the classic Johann Wyss novel, Swiss Family Treehouse is the desert island home of the castaway Robinson clan. Reached by a 75-foot suspension bridge, the fantastic treetop dwelling contains bedrooms, a family room complete with pump organ, and an ingenious water supply system. The tree and its stairways and rooms are actually an intricately designed and engineered *building*, subject to the same strict safety and building codes as the other structures at Walt Disney World. The steel, concrete, and stucco "tree" has foundation "roots" 42 feet deep and is covered with 800,000 fabricated leaves, flowers, and buds—but is also draped with living Spanish moss. The *Disneyodendron* (Disney tree) is one of the rarest botanical forms in the world—only four are known to exist, one each in Anaheim, Florida, Tokyo, and Paris.

Adjacent to the Swiss Family Treehouse is the Jungle Cruise, a popular attraction from Disneyland, adapted for the Magic Kingdom. The Jungle Cruise was the brainchild of designer Harper Goff, who had served as an art director on Disney's 1954 classic *20,000 Leagues Under the Sea* and contributed many important ideas to that movie. Goff was fond of the 1952 Humphrey Bogart/Katharine Hepburn film *The African Queen* and thought that the waterway adventures and animals depicted in the film could be readily adapted for a ride-through attraction. Although guests are spared the bickering of Charlie Alnutt and Rose Sayer, they do board a familiar canopied jungle launch, from which they view a geographically amalgamated 10-minute safari along the Irrawaddy River of Burma (Myanmar), Cambodia's Mekong, the Egyptian Nile, the African Congo, and the rapids of Kilimanjaro. Sights along the rivers include long-abandoned temples, native villages, and many animal denizens of the jungle, such as lions, giraffes, hippos, and elephants—all portrayed by Disney-Imagineered stand-ins for the real thing. (It is legend that Walt Disney wanted real animals for the Jungle Cruise, but learned that most of the beasts would shy away from display areas or sleep during daylight hours.)

Across the jungle path is a distinctly different "animal show," Tropical Serenade. Housed in a dramatic, towering thatched-roof pagoda, it is similar to the prototype Audio-Animatronics show, the Enchanted Tiki Room, which premiered at Disneyland in 1963. In the show dozens of parrots, macaws, and

*Exotic sights from the rivers of the world await hardy explorers on the Jungle Cruise.*

TOP:
*Zazu from* The Lion King *is slated to host an updated version of Tropical Serenade.*

CENTER:
*The landscaping of a profusion of tropical plants greatly increases the kinetic feel of Adventureland.*

BOTTOM:
*The popular Pirates of the Caribbean opened in Caribbean Plaza in late 1973.*

cockatoos join in a boisterous musical program with fountains, singing flowers, tiki statues, and a climactic tropical thunderstorm. Plans are in the works for the wisecracking parrot Iago from *Aladdin* and the prissy hornbill Zazu from *The Lion King* to host an updated version of this popular show.

Throughout Adventureland, clothing, trinkets, and souvenirs from Africa, Asia, and the South Seas are sold in a variety of themed gift shops, boutiques, and carts. Thematic dining is available at locales such as the Sunshine Tree Terrace and El Pirata y el Perico (The Pirate and the Parrot).

The first major expansion of the Magic Kingdom was an extension of Adventureland in December 1973, called Caribbean Plaza. This area houses the favorite Disneyland attraction Pirates of the Caribbean, translated for the Magic Kingdom with a few changes to the overall layout, as prescribed by operational and aesthetic dictates. Caribbean Plaza also provides a transition from a Spanish plaza on the northwest side of Adventureland to the Spanish-influenced architectural styles of the 1850s American Southwest in the southwest corner of Frontierland.

## MOVING WEST: FRONTIERLAND

Frontierland is probably the most distinctly American statement in the Magic Kingdom, a tribute to the pioneer spirit that moved Americans westward from the 1770s to the 1880s. It pays homage to many American frontiers, from the old South to the mighty Mississippi to the desert Southwest.

The buildings near the Plaza entrance to Frontierland are reminiscent of St. Louis in the 1840s, when this booming Missouri town marked the end of the East and the beginning of the frontier. The Diamond Horseshoe Saloon recalls the velvet-draped dance-halls of the day, and the interior stage boasts a house curtain in the style of Toulouse-Lautrec, created by John de Cuir, Sr., an Academy Award–winning art director. As Frontierland moves west, so does the geographic inspiration for its decor. Gold leaf and neatly painted side walls give way to board sidewalks and weathered clapboards.

Grizzly Hall is a Northwoods union hall that houses one of the Magic Kingdom's favorite (and silliest) attractions, Country Bear Jamboree. Inside, a beautifully designed and skillfully programmed cast of Audio-Animatronics bruins puts on a foot-stompin', back-slappin', happy hoedown. Originally conceived by Disney legend Marc Davis, based on a suggestion by Walt Disney himself, Country Bear Jamboree was envisioned for a proposed Disney recreation and real estate development in Mineral King, California. When that project fell through, the show was brought to life in the Magic Kingdom, and it is so popular that there is invariably a hefty wait to see it. (When the Country Bear Jamboree was exported to Disneyland in 1972, Disney designers built two duplicate theaters, so that twice as many people could see the show. Sadly, whether due to the attraction's location or audience taste, the California Jamboree has never been as popular, and the second theater is rarely used.)

## THE MANY IDENTITIES OF DISCOVERY ISLAND

On the initial flyover visits of the Florida property that would become Walt Disney World, Walt Disney became enamored of a picturesque little island in the middle of Bay Lake. It was this natural body of water with its charming 11-acre isle that inspired Walt Disney to order this corner of the property to be developed first.

Walt Disney probably didn't know the colorful history of the island, nor could he have imagined the evolution it would undergo in a short quarter-century. From 1900 to 1937 it was called Raz Island after the family that lived and farmed on it. In the late 1930s Delmar Nicholson (known as Radio Nick) purchased the island for $800 to make a home for his family. Radio Nick was an outdoorsman, botanist, civic leader, and Florida's first radio disc jockey. For more than 20 years Nick, his wife, and their pet sandhill crane lived on the island, which Nick called Idle Bay Isle. Nick and his wife grew many varieties of fruits and greenery, which they sold to local markets. Ill health forced Nick to sell the island, and a group of local businesspeople purchased it as a hunting retreat. Disney purchased the island in 1965.

When Walt Disney World opened in 1971, the island was renamed Blackbeard's Island, but remained undeveloped. In 1974 Buena Vista Construction Company began developing the island by transporting 50,000 cubic yards of soil to build up its central acreage. The name Blackbeard's Island was changed to Treasure Island, and the theme of a pirate's hideaway, with shipwrecks and buried treasure, was established. With initial construction completed, Treasure Island opened on April 7, 1974.

The island was closed from January through March of 1976 for a major renovation and for construction of the Thirsty Perch (a snack bar) and the Avian Way (a walk-through aviary). When the island reopened on April 1, it was renamed Discovery Island and featured many exotic birds and plants. In June 1978 the American alligator and the Galápagos tortoise exhibits were added. In 1979, after meeting specific requirements in education, conservation, entertainment, and research, Discovery Island was granted accreditation by the American Zoo and Aquarium Association.

But Discovery Island is more than an attraction featuring birds and plants. The staff is dedicated to the preservation and breeding of these magnificent animals. Over the years, many of the species on the island have reproduced successfully, including cranes, toucans, and flamingos. During the first four years on Discovery Island, many rare birds were bred. The facility has received considerable public notice for the first captive breeding of the Toco toucan, and it was nominated for an award from the American Zoo and Aquarium Association for raising more than 25 scarlet ibis in captivity. Discovery Island was only the second place in North America to successfully raise the rhinoceros hornbill, and in 1991 it became the first place in the world to successfully raise Maguari storks in captivity.

Accredited zoos work together to conserve species, and toward that end will loan birds to associate zoos or aviaries for breeding. The island participates in four Species Survival Plans for endangered animals, through which the animals are managed collectively among zoos for the welfare of the species. More than 100 animal species (including some injured brown pelicans and southern bald eagles that could not survive on their own) and 250 plant species inhabit this lush island paradise.

Accessible only by boat, Discovery Island is one of the most easily overlooked, but most rewarding, destinations in Walt Disney World.

## FORT WILDERNESS

Right between the Magic Kingdom and Epcot, near the shores of Bay Lake, is one of Walt Disney World's most surprising resorts, providing a unique, quiet, relaxed escape into 750 acres of pine and cypress woods and wilderness, crisscrossed with canals. Disney's Fort Wilderness Resort and Campground, which opened in 1991, is ranked among the finest in the world. In fact, there are so many activities available at Fort Wilderness—two heated swimming pools, nightly hayrides, horseback trail riding, a petting farm, pony rides, bicycle riding, lighted tennis courts, lake and canal fishing, playgrounds, nature walks, jogging trails, volleyball, tetherball, basketball, game room arcades, sailing, shuffleboard, canoeing, pedal boats, lake swimming, water skiing—that it's possible to spend a week there without even *thinking* of a theme park.

In April 1974 Pioneer Hall opened at Fort Wilderness, housing Crockett's Tavern, a full-service lounge and dinner restaurant featuring wall-to-wall, floor-to-ceiling Davy Crockett memorabilia, and the Trail's End Buffeteria (the Disney word for cafeteria). The main attraction at Pioneer Hall is the long-running "Hoop-Dee-Doo Musical Revue" Dinner Show, which features an all-you-can-eat home-style supper and a Western musical-comedy revue.

Old-time steam trains chugged through the woods of the Fort Wilderness Campground beginning in 1973. A form of interior transportation for campers, they were eventually decommissioned in 1977. Part of the track can still be seen around the campground, and some of the cars were adapted for other uses at Pleasure Island and Disneyland Paris.

There are 784 private campsites, ranging in length from 25 to 65 feet and spaced throughout 20 camping loops. All are buffered by lush wilderness and feature running water, 110/220-volt electrical outlets, sewer connections, charcoal grills, picnic tables and paved driveway pads. All sites are close to air-conditioned comfort stations with laundry facilities, as well as trading posts, recreational areas, and transportation.

If you'd treasure a weekend in the woods, but don't know a pup tent from a pop gun, there are 408 wilderness homes, each 500 square feet, sleeping up to six and featuring air conditioning, color TV, a telephone, and a kitchen fully equipped with electric range, refrigerator, dishwasher, microwave, cooking utensils, and dishes—plus daily housekeeping services. Each private, wooded home site has an outdoor grill and a picnic table.

Fort Wilderness achieved the highest rating from Trailer Life Campground/RV Services. (It is one of only five U.S. locations to receive this rating.)

To the north of Grizzly Hall, the Rivers of America wind their way into the wilderness. The inviting half-mile-long waterway, with its variety of watercraft (including keelboats, canoes, rafts, and a paddle-wheel riverboat), evokes the days when the river was a true highway. The iconic riverboat, the *Richard F. Irvine*, is an authentic, functional stern-wheeler steamboat, built in dry-dock at Walt Disney World and launched in 1973. The steamboat departs from the Liberty Square Landing at the southeast edge of the waterway.

The Rivers of America flow around Tom Sawyer Island, which opened in 1973. Based on the similarly named area of Disneyland, Tom Sawyer Island is a paean to the barefoot boy, a playground of caves, rocks, footpaths, a barrel bridge, a suspension bridge, and even a frontier outpost, Fort Sam Clemens. Access to the island is by river raft only, and combined with its rugged landscape, this gives it a marvelous feeling of remoteness and solitude.

Beyond the Rivers of America, the landscape becomes distinctly arid, and the 197-foot butte of Big Thunder Mountain Railroad looms. Based on a popular Disneyland attraction, Big Thunder Mountain (dedicated in November 1980) was the first major addition to the Walt Disney World Frontierland. In some ways, Big Thunder was *returning* to the Magic Kingdom, since its conceptual precursor, Thunder Mesa, had been designed

*Like modern-day Tom Sawyers, Magic Kingdom visitors cross the mighty river.*

## DISNEY MEETS THE OLE SWIMMIN' HOLE: RIVER COUNTRY

Long before the proliferation of freeway-adjacent water parks, with their exposed structural supports, impersonal scale, and cold aquamarine fiberglass chutes, Disney designers created River Country, a deceptively bucolic water park, inspired by the childhood pastimes of Mark Twain's Mississippi River wilderness. River Country, which opened in June 1976, is the Disney version of an old-fashioned swimmin' hole; it is located on the edge of Bay Lake in Fort Wilderness Campground.

The grounds are grassy and inviting, a boardwalk creates a nature trail through a cypress swamp, a wide beach invites sunbathers, and the swimming areas feature flume and raft rides. Two water slides shoot swimmers into the 300,000-gallon pool at about seven feet above the surface of the water. Bay Cove, the swimming hole (actually a natural part of Bay Lake), is equipped with rope swings, a ship's boom, and other jumping-off points for would-be Huck Finns.

The park gets its water supply from an intake/filter pipe in Bay Lake. Water is sent along the lake bottom into a pump system inside River Country's artificial mountain. From there, it is forced down the flume troughs at about 8,500 gallons per minute, providing water for the flumes and continually replenishing River Country's water supply. Separating the park's water from regular lake water is a large rubber "bladder," which remains inflated six inches above the surface of Bay Lake with the help of a specialized sensor system.

More than a decade after it opened, the ongoing popularity—and limited capacity—of River Country led to the construction of Typhoon Lagoon and Blizzard Beach water parks.

ABOVE:
*At Splash Mountain passengers riding in "hollowed-out" log boats experience the steepest flume drop in the world, plummeting 52 feet at a 45-degree angle, at speeds up to 40 miles per hour.*

RIGHT:
*Crooning Audio-Animatronics Alligator figures are part of the show inside Splash Mountain—a collection of the stories from the animated sequences of Disney's* Song of the South *(1946).*

PREVIOUS PAGES:
*The steamboat passing Liberty Square Landing at dusk.*

to enlarge the Florida Frontierland. Big Thunder, like its predecessor Space Mountain (located in Tomorrowland), addressed the modern audience's need for a thrill ride—and, of couse, Disney designers couldn't put up *just* a roller coaster. Big Thunder is a roller coaster wrapped in a stunning Monument Valley landscape, using runaway mine trains, and layered with the Gold Rush story of boom and bust in the town of Tumbleweed. The dressing of this attraction includes 20 Audio-Animatronics figures, from chickens and possums to a rainmaker known as Professor Cumulus Isobar. Lending authenticity to the surroundings is antique mining equipment, including an ore crusher, a mining flume, and an ore-hauling wagon. These once-functional pieces were purchased by Disney prop scouts on travels throughout the American Southwest.

In 1992 the original Frontierland Station, which had opened in May 1972, was demolished and a new depot was incorporated into the overall attraction design. Just past the new Frontierland Railroad Station is another mountain in the Magic Kingdom range, Splash Mountain, which opened in July 1992. The mountain, also known as Chickapin Hill, and its terraced red-earth slopes are reminiscent of the storybook Georgia portrayed in the 1946 Disney feature *Song of the South*. The saturated colors of the design are based on those created for the film by Claude Coats and Mary Blair. Much as Big Thunder Mountain and Space Mountain took the standard roller coaster and elevated them to a Disney theme park spectacular, Splash Mountain essentially takes a log-flume ride to unprecedented heights of design and engineering. The storyline, which unfolds through complex Audio-Animatronics tableaux as guests float by in hollowed-out log boats, is an amalgamation of the animated sequences of *Song of the South*, with Brer Fox and Brer Bear in pursuit of Brer Rabbit. As the fox throws Brer Rabbit into the briar patch, the log boats plummet 52 feet at a 45-degree angle, at speeds up to 40 miles per hour—the steepest flume drop in the world.

## ON TO LIBERTY SQUARE

Frontierland gives way on the northeast to Liberty Square, an adjunct historical "land" built especially for the Magic Kingdom—but initially proposed for Disneyland. In 1958 part of an announced expansion of Disneyland included two new areas to the east of Main Street, Edison Square and Liberty Street. Though these areas have not been built in the California park, no idea is ever wasted at Walt Disney Imagineering, and the Liberty Street concept and its keynote attraction, The Hall of Presidents, were added to the initial designs for Florida's Magic Kingdom.

The Hall of Presidents was first conceived to present the story of the American Revolution in an entertaining and understandable way, but without diminishing its critical historical importance. The centerpiece of this show was to have been a proscenium theater presenting all of the United States presidents as life-size Audio-Animatronics. The only problem with this idea was that at the time it was too far ahead of the technology available to execute

TOP:
*This new Frontierland Station replaced the original depot during construction of Splash Mountain in 1992.*

BOTTOM:
*Big Thunder Mountain is a striking Monument Valley–style landscape, steeped in the Gold Rush legend.*

ABOVE:
*Liberty Square in a detailed concept painting* (TOP) *and with the majestic Liberty Tree.*

RIGHT:
*President Clinton addresses The Hall of Presidents, the first president after Lincoln to have a "speaking role" in the attraction.*

OPPOSITE TOP:
*A phantom at the keyboard issues mournful music and wailing spirits from a majestic pipe organ in The Haunted Mansion.*

OPPOSITE BOTTOM:
*The dark, brooding exterior of the mansion recalls gothic residences of the Hudson River Valley.*

it. In 1958 the Audio-Animatronics system was barely crawling, and this ambitious show required much more sophisticated presentation than it could provide. Work continued over the next few years on a prototype president for the hall, Abraham Lincoln.

An impromptu viewing of this figure under construction by the head of the 1964–65 New York World's Fair led to an accelerated development of the technology, and Great Moments with Mr. Lincoln was created for the fair. The popular attraction was also installed in the Main Street Opera House at Disneyland in 1965, and since the technology was by then tried and true, The Hall of Presidents was added to the list of attractions for the upcoming Walt Disney World Magic Kingdom. Sculptor Blaine Gibson has been primarily responsible for the presidential cast of characters, and he has even interrupted his retirement to sculpt presidents Ronald Reagan, George Bush, and Bill Clinton.

The Hall of Presidents show was refurbished and updated in late 1993, with a refined presentation showcasing the framing of the Constitution with a new narration read by Maya Angelou, as well as a reading by the *actual* president of the United States, Bill Clinton. The Audio-Animatronics Clinton shares the stage with all his predecessors, reciting a speech written by Imagineers Justin Segal, Tom Fitzgerald, and Rick Rothschild; lyricist Tim Rice; Walt Disney Imagineering vice chairman Marty Sklar; Disney CEO Michael Eisner; and Clinton speechwriter Jonathan Prince. The audio was recorded in the White House library.

Outside The Hall of Presidents stands a majestic live oak (*Quercus virginiana*)—the Liberty Tree. The tree commemorates the communal meeting place of the Sons of Liberty, and it is decorated with 13 lanterns, representing the 13 original colonies. The tree itself was transplanted from the southern edge of the Walt Disney World property and then had a second, younger oak grafted onto it at the base in order to enhance its impressive shape and presence.

To the east of The Hall of Presidents is The Haunted Mansion. The mansion's interior show is quite similar to the Disneyland original—an almost disquietingly lighthearted paranormal house tour, much of which is viewed from podlike OmniMover vehicles called Doom Buggies, which travel on a single-rail track. The mansion contains spectacular settings and many amazing special effects, as well as exquisite tableau ghost gags by Disney masters Marc Davis, Claude Coats, and Ken Anderson. Where the exterior of the Disneyland mansion is that of a light, graceful, filigreed antebellum plantation house, the Florida mansion is a brooding—almost architecturally menacing—dark brick and stone gothic, reminiscent of the great mansions of the Hudson River Valley.

FANTASYLAND

Over the wooden footbridge to the east of Liberty Square is the central Plaza, and to the north rise the towering spires of Cinderella Castle. This is the entrance to the archetypal Disney realm of the Magic Kingdom, Fantasyland. In Fantasyland the Disney characters of motion pictures comfortably find a home, within the stout walls of a fairy-tale castle, in the atmosphere of a medieval tournament.

*Inside the castle the Cinderella story is vividly recounted in five huge mosaic tile murals in the entry corridor.*

OPPOSITE:
*Beneath the night-lit Cinderella Castle is Cinderella's Golden Carrousel.*

The Cinderella motif is carried through not only in the castle form, but also in architectural ornamentation, which uses characters from the film, and in a spectacular series of mosaic tile murals in the entry corridor. The murals, designed by Imagineer Dorothea Redmond and executed by mosaicist Hanns-Joachim Scharff, tell the story of Cinderella in five 15-by-10-foot panels. In the entry courtyard of the castle, a delicate bronze statue of Cinderella with her mouse and bird friends perches on the basin of a fountain. Among the many things that set the Disney designers apart is the ability to focus on just such items. Although they serve no operational function, through their superb and imaginative craftsmanship they delight and entrance and help tell the Cinderella story.

The Cinderella motif culminates at Cinderella's Golden Carrousel. The carousel, which was built in 1917, was found by Disney scouts in the now-closed Olympic Park in Maplewood, New Jersey. Naturally, it required extensive "Disneyfication" to bring it up to show standards. Many of the wooden horses were replaced with fiberglass replicas. The steeds were re-posed to make them charge instead of canter. The story of Cinderella is represented in 18 hand-painted scenes on the wooden canopy above the horses.

The Sword in the Stone, of Arthurian legend and the subject of a 1963 Disney animated feature, was added to the forecourt of Cinderella's Golden Carrousel in 1994. Here, in a daily ceremony, Merlin supervises the selection of the juvenile monarchs of the Magic Kingdom from crowds of hopeful park guests.

CLOCKWISE FROM RIGHT:
*The Mad Tea Party whirls with huge crazy-colored, teacups; passengers meet some devilish characters during Mr. Toad's Wild Ride; Snow White is menaced by the jealous queen in Snow White's Adventures; a night flight over London to Never Land awaits passengers of Peter Pan's Flight; a monolithic Mr. Toad adjusts his monocle for a better view of Fantasyland.*

On the Magic Kingdom's opening day, Fantasyland favorites direct from Disneyland made up the bulk of the attractions. In the Mad Tea Party, themed to the 1951 animated feature *Alice in Wonderland*, passengers board oversize, crazy-colored spinning teacups. The Mad Tea Party is much like its California cousin, but is enhanced by a canopy roof for protection from inclement weather.

The "dark rides" are so called because they course through the dark under black light. The sets and props are painted with fluorescent paints, and the resulting effect is reminiscent of the vibrant colors of animation. These dark rides include Mr. Toad's Wild Ride, an automotive romp to Nowhere in Particular; Peter Pan's Flight, a moonlit flight over London and Never Land; and Snow White's Adventures, a scary flight through Snow White's haunted forest to the cottage of the Seven Dwarfs. This attraction was completely refurbished and upgraded in 1995.

Dumbo, the Flying Elephant, another Disneyland attraction, is a circling herd of 10 flying elephant cabs, which are individually piloted by their

LEFT:
*Maestro Mickey led an all-Disney Audio-Animatronics orchestra in the Mickey Mouse Revue, relocated to Tokyo Disneyland in the early 1980s.*

human navigators. In 1993 the original attraction was replaced with a completely re-Imagineered version, which added redesigned elephants, increased the herd to 16, and upgraded the decorative setting based upon a design created for Disneyland Paris.

The Magic Kingdom has always featured performances by beloved Disney characters. The Mickey Mouse Revue was an all-new theater show created for the Magic Kingdom in 1971. This Audio-Animatronics show featured musical performances by 60 classic Disney characters, singing and playing favorite Disney tunes such as "Zip-a-Dee-Doo-Dah" and "Who's Afraid of the Big Bad Wolf," all under the baton of Maestro Mickey Mouse. The Mickey Mouse Revue was removed in September 1980 and relocated to Tokyo Disneyland, where it remains one of that park's most popular attractions. The Mickey Mouse Revue theater remained vacant for several years, until the opening of *Captain EO* in EPCOT Center displaced the original 3-D presentation there, *Magic Journeys*, which moved into the Mickey Mouse Revue theater in December 1987. The pre-show for *Magic Journeys* was the classic 1953 Chip n' Dale 3-D short cartoon *Working for Peanuts. Magic Journeys* was cleared again in December 1993, in preparation for the Legend of the Lion King show.

In July 1994, shortly after the theatrical release of the animated feature *The Lion King*, the Legend of the Lion King show, presented by Kodak, opened. This complex presentation uses film clips, in-theater lighting and effects, sophisticated puppets, and a thundering sound system to completely envelop the 500-person audience in the story, sights, and sounds of *The Lion King*, including the musical sequences "Circle of Life," "Hakuna Matata," "Can You Feel the Love Tonight?" and "I Just Can't Wait to Be King." The attraction is similar to Voyage of the Little Mermaid at Disney-MGM Studios, in that it is a unique—and uniquely Disney—hybrid of entertainment media.

ABOVE:
*The 16 circling elephants are individually piloted by their human navigators on Dumbo, the Flying Elephant* (TOP)*; Timon and Pumbaa present their story in the Legend of the Lion King* (BOTTOM).

*It's a Small World is a delightful around-the-world tour through the eyes of children, originally created for the 1964–65 New York World's Fair.*

*Based on Disney's classic 1954 science fiction film, 20,000 Leagues Under the Sea was an exciting "undersea" adventure, but the attraction closed in 1994.*

It's a Small World, presented by Mattel, has become such an iconic (often in a ridiculous sense) Disney theme park attraction that a thoughtful examination of its detail is rare. Developed on a crash schedule for the UNICEF pavilion at the 1964–65 New York World's Fair, the attraction features a colorful and fancifully rendered around-the-world tour through the eyes of children. The brilliant graphics and color stylings of Mary Blair were at full flower in the original (now located at Disneyland), and Blair was one of the key designers who updated and enhanced the show for its Magic Kingdom version. The signature tune was created by Richard M. Sherman and Robert B. Sherman—the first version of the Small World show that they saw featured a noisy collision of international anthems. They simplified this discord into a simple roundelay that could be sung in several languages and orchestrated on several instrument types simultaneously, to create individual sonic tableaux without a painful overall cacophony. It's a Small World has also been re-created for Tokyo Disneyland and Disneyland Paris.

The storyline and distinctive Victorian styling of Disney's classic 1954 science fiction film were used to create an "undersea" adventure with the same name: 20,000 Leagues Under the Sea. The Submarine Voyage attraction has been a favorite at Disneyland since 1959. Due to its labor-intensive operation and maintenance, however, Walt Disney World's 20,000 Leagues Under the Sea had to be closed until further notice in 1994.

### MICKEY'S STARLAND

Mickey's Starland, adjacent to Fantasyland, was built as Mickey's Birthdayland and opened June 18, 1988, in celebration of Mickey's 60th birthday. Guests at the Magic Kingdom boarded a special Birthday Express to the new Birthdayland Station, where a cartoony celebration in colorful "tent" buildings honored

Mickey, and guests had a controlled opportunity to greet and take their pictures with the Mouse himself. The area proved so popular—particularly with young children—that although it had been intended as temporary, it remained open as Mickey's Starland. Its popularity was not lost on Disney Imagineers, who expanded on the concept when they developed Mickey's Toontown for Disneyland in 1990. In 1996 the Imagineers redesigned the original Mickey's Starland area with the introduction of country-style dwellings for Mickey and his friends, who have ostensibly joined together to celebrate the arrival of Mickey's Toontown Fair. For young children, a highlight is the Barnstormer, a pint-sized roller coaster ride in old-fashioned cars that look like airplanes.

*An artist's rendering of the house of Mickey Mouse in Mickey's Starland* (TOP) *is translated to dimensional reality in the Magic Kingdom* (BOTTOM).

# VILLAGE RESORT

Plans for the first permanent residential complex on Walt Disney World property—Lake Buena Vista—were announced in June 1973 and called for four different themed recreational communities: Golf, Tennis, Boating, and Western, all with townhouses, tennis courts, and swimming pools.

A more detailed announcement came in May 1974: 53 townhouses had been completed, bringing the total to 133. Four model homes had also been finished, and construction of a shopping center, Lake Buena Vista Village, was underway. Sixty treehouse-style homes were also under construction. Lake Buena Vista Communities, Inc., was set to work on single-family residences, apartment buildings, and condominiums at a later date.

In July 1974 a construction contract was awarded for residential development of an adult retirement community, a complex of vacation townhouses, and residential apartments. And in October 1975 the completion of the 60-unit Treehouse Village was announced. But by this time, there was no longer any discussion of their sale as residences or the sale of any of the other Lake Buena Vista properties.

The following year a relaxing waterside collection of shops called the Lake Buena Vista Shopping Village (renamed Walt Disney World Village, now known as the Disney Village Marketplace) had its opening.

So what happened to the burgeoning community of Lake Buena Vista? Maintaining the municipality of Lake Buena Vista with on-site permanent residents presented governmental dilemmas—taxation being one, but *voting rights* being the most crucial. Given the structure of government of the Walt Disney World property, these residents would have had voting rights regarding expansion of the property and development of the Magic Kingdom.

The complex became Walt Disney World Village Resort in 1985 and Disney Village Resort in 1989. Most of the Lake Buena Vista development was folded into The Disney Institute in 1995.

Although five Disney-owned hotels were planned for the Magic Kingdom area in the first five years of the resort, only three were built during that time period. Adjacent to the Lake Buena Vista development, however, a series of hotels not owned by the Disney company, but located within the boundaries of Walt Disney World and designated official hotels, opened in 1972 and early 1973.

The Americana Dutch Inn (10/72, renamed Grosvenor Resort), Hotel Royal Plaza (10/72), Travelodge (11/72, known as Viscount from 1984 to 1989), and Howard Johnson (2/73, changed to Courtyard by Marriott in 1995) formed the Motor Plaza Inn (later known as Hotel Plaza). The Buena Vista Palace and the Hilton opened in 1983, followed in 1987 by the Pickett Suite (renamed Guest Quarters Suite, then remodeled and renamed Doubletree Guest Suite Resort in 1995). This cluster of hotels is now an unofficial extension of the Disney Village, known as Disney Village Hotel Plaza.

Of all the realms in the Magic Kingdom, the most troublesome and most frequently altered is Tomorrowland. Predicting the future has always been problematic, but never more so than in the late 20th century. It is not just a matter of *imagining* things to come; the real problem is presenting these concepts in permanent facilities with shows of lasting appeal. Even when Disneyland opened in 1955, Tomorrowland had become so dated that Walt Disney spearheaded major renovations that premiered in 1959 and 1967.

The initial Tomorrowland at the Magic Kingdom drew on the Disneyland version but heightened its coldly dramatic architectural approach, in keeping with the movie futurism of the time. At its 1971 opening, the manned flight to the moon was barely two years past, and the horizons of space travel appeared limitless. The same technology that had put men on the moon promised sparkling new cities and limitless opportunities for humankind—and for Imagineers.

From the Skyway, a gondola tramway between Tomorrowland and Fantasyland, passengers have gained a bird's-eye view of the Magic Kingdom since 1971. This Florida attraction has outlived the Disneyland original that inspired it, which was demolished in 1994.

The Grand Prix Raceway is a sleeker, speedier take on the popular Autopia attraction at Disneyland. Scale-size race cars are dispatched by pit attendants into four lanes of racing (at an average speed of seven miles per hour) on a 2,260-foot-long track patterned after typical Grand Prix courses. (In 1988 the raceway track was slightly relocated and shortened to accommodate construction of Mickey's Birthdayland.)

Opened on November 28, 1974, the StarJets (replaced by Astro Orbiter in 1994) were both a visual icon and an attraction; operationally they were more akin to the Dumbo ride in Fantasyland than anything else. Groups

OPPOSITE:
*Sixty pedestal-mounted treetop homes, called treehouses, were completed at Lake Buena Vista in October 1975.*

BELOW:
*Futuristic cityscape meets exposition in a mid-1970s concept painting of Tomorrowland. The gleaming cleanliness and austere architectural lines reflect the mind-set of futurism in the days of the moon shots and Stanley Kubrick's* 2001: A Space Odyssey. *To the far left is the Grand Prix Raceway, and to the far right the Carousel of Progress with Space Mountain towering behind, in the center.*

*In Tomorrowland you once could blast off in your own personal StarJet and whirl around a Saturn V–type rocket, in a journey evocative of the 1960s space race.*

of two-passenger StarJets circled a central pylon styled after a Saturn V rocket; the pilots could control the height of the cabs up to 80 feet above the ground.

Circle-Vision 360 opened in November 1971. (The basic Circle-Vision 360 system had debuted as Circarama at Disneyland in 1955.) Circle-Vision motion pictures are shot with nine 35mm cameras mounted on a circular rig. Screened from nine projectors in a specially designed theater-in-the-round, the films literally surround viewers with sight and multichannel sound. This format is exhibited at Disneyland, the Walt Disney World Magic Kingdom, Epcot, Tokyo Disneyland, Disneyland Paris, and international fairs and expos. *America the Beautiful*, made for Disneyland in 1967, was the premiere presentation at the Magic Kingdom Circle-Vision 360. An all-new film, *Magic Carpet 'Round the World*, premiered in 1974. A new, updated version of *America the Beautiful* ran from 1975 to 1979; *Magic Carpet 'Round the World* returned from 1979 to 1984; and *American Journeys* premiered in 1984.

In December 1971, when Flight to the Moon belatedly premiered, its fantasy presentation of a moon trip seemed rather weak in comparison to the recent real space travel that most guests had witnessed right from their living rooms. It was replaced in June 1975 by the updated, extremely factual—and somewhat dry—Mission to Mars.

Another kind of flight, commercial jet flight, was the focus of If You Had Wings, which opened in June 1972. Film, music, three-dimensional sets, and speed effects took guests in OmniMover vehicles (a similar system to the

## THE GOLF RESORT / THE DISNEY INN / SHADES OF GREEN

Golf and Walt Disney World have been linked since the World began. The championship Palm and Magnolia golf courses, which have hosted the Walt Disney World Golf Classic since their opening in 1971, became the site of one of the most restful Walt Disney World resorts.

Opened in December 1973, The Golf Resort was an intimate 125-room resort, located off the monorail route but adjacent to the Magic Kingdom. Surrounded by the woods, lawns, and fields of the two golf courses, the resort had a lush and secluded appeal and an intimacy of service unlike any of the other resort properties. It's not surprising to learn that many of the Walt Disney Productions, WED Enterprises, and Walt Disney Attractions executives were avid golfers. In February 1986, another 150 guest rooms were added to the resort, and its name was changed to The Disney Inn (because research revealed that many guests thought that the resort was a golfers-only retreat).

The Disney Inn was leased from Disney in February 1994 and purchased outright in 1996—believe it or not—military downsizing. Since more and more military personnel are stationed stateside, having affordable recreational opportunities is considered necessary for morale. Renamed Shades of Green, the inn is open only to active, retired, and reserve members of the armed services and civilian employees of the military. The army runs similar hotels in South Korea, Germany, and Hawaii, but Shades of Green is the first such operation in the continental United States. It is staffed by non-Disney civilians and is self-supporting.

## CONTEMPORARY RESORT

Along with Cinderella Castle, the sleek A-frame structure of the Contemporary Resort was one of the first icons of the new Walt Disney World. One of five major resort hotels planned for Walt Disney World's five-year Phase One, the Contemporary was designed by Welton Becket and Associates of California and WED Enterprises; the structural engineer was Richard Bradshaw, Inc., and construction was done by U.S. Steel Realty Development, a susidiary of United States Steel Corporation.

A unique construction method, called unitized modular construction, was used. The process began with the building of a superstructure of thirteen 150-foot-high steel-trussed A-frames (by the American Bridge Division of U.S. Steel). Individual guest rooms, manufactured in a special plant located three miles from the site, were then slid into the existing structural frame. Once assembled, the structure was covered by a specially designed sun-resistant glass called Solar Bronze.

The interior of the superstructure created a grand 14-story concourse, dubbed the Grand Canyon Concourse, and themed to the American Southwest. The Walt Disney World Monorail System runs directly through the concourse, entering at the fourth-floor level, and the arrival and departure of the trains brings a kinetic grandeur to an already spectacular space. Adding to the visual appeal of this space is a large mural designed by Mary Blair.

The main hotel structure and the two Garden Wings that flank it have 1,041 guest rooms; there are also seven shops, two snack bars, two lounges, convention space, a marina, a beach, a health club, and two swimming pools.

In fall 1991 a new Convention Center was added in a separate building; it is attached to the original structure by an enclosed walkway which leads to the original convention space on the second floor. This new facility contains more than 90,000 square feet of meeting space.

Doom Buggies of The Haunted Mansion) from the Magic Kingdom to ports of call around the world. If You Had Wings was updated and renamed If You Could Fly in 1987, then superseded in June 1989 by Dreamflight. The new attraction retained the theme of commercial flight and the OmniMover track layout, but replaced the show with whimsical views of the adventure and romance of air travel, from a giant pop-up book view of early barnstormers, to the elegance of the China Clipper M-130 Flying Boat.

RIGHT:
*A concept drawing by Herbert Ryman shows a looming, free-form structure for Space Mountain.*

BELOW:
*The finished Space Mountain has straightened some of the artist's free-form lines, but it is no less grandly futuristic.*

The mid-1970s were a time of perpetual expansion for Tomorrowland, which became a veritable sonic boomtown. For several years, Disney had toyed with the idea of a thrill ride. Inspiration came from Walt Disney himself. In 1959 Walt had pushed through Matterhorn Mountain at Disneyland, replete with schussing bobsled run (a roller coaster). Space Mountain was another of Walt's concepts, an indoor roller coaster in the dark. The idea was ultimately executed for the Magic Kingdom and opened after 10 years of development, on January 15, 1974. The distinctive exterior of Space Mountain, presented by FedEx, is a marvel of pre-stressed concrete and steel, towering nearly 175 feet above the ground (and descending 15 feet beneath it). The intricate side-by-side track system is one of the earliest computer-aided designs. Guests board tandem-seat rockets, which blast into space, dipping and turning at high speeds through a starry cosmos. Since the coaster is in the dark, the riders can't see the guide rails and experience a loss of orientation that increases the sense of motion. The Florida Space Mountain was followed by a smaller, single-track version at Disneyland in 1977.

Carousel of Progress came to Tomorrowland in 1975. Created for the General Electric Progressland pavilion at the 1964–65 New York World's Fair, the carousel show uses Audio-Animatronics and a unique 250-seat theater that revolves around a central stage. Carousel of Progress depicted a typical American family from 1880 to 1965 and the influence of electricity in the home. In 1967 the carousel was installed in Disneyland and happily spun through Tomorrowland until it was moved to Walt Disney World. The show didn't move intact, though; it was retrofitted with a new theme and a new song. "There's a Great Big Beautiful Tomorrow," the original show's upbeat anthem of progress, was replaced with a new (and decidedly guarded) Sherman brothers tune, "Now Is the Best Time of Your Life." In 1994 the entire carousel show was again renovated, this time returning it to a world of "future past," with the restoration of the original show theme song, and the whole proceeding dedicated to the visionary intuition of Walt Disney. With this latest renovation, the attraction was renamed *Walt Disney's* Carousel of Progress. According to Disney publicity, Carousel of Progress has been seen by more people than any other single theater show in American history.

The new WEDWay PeopleMover—an updated version of the PeopleMover (installed at Disneyland in 1967)—opened at the Magic Kingdom on July 1, 1975. This new system used a technology of linear induction. Electricity flowing through field coils embedded in the WEDWay track attracts steel platens on the bases of passenger vehicles, pulling them forward. When a vehicle has passed over a magnetized motor, the electricity in that motor switches off. The vehicle continues on, magnetically pulled down the track by the subsequent motors. A more recent generation of this technology made its inaugural run at the Houston International Airport in Texas during 1981. The WEDWay PeopleMover received a commendation for design achievement from the National Endowment for the Arts and the United States Department of Transportation.

TOP TO BOTTOM:
*The most recent renovation of the Carousel of Progress; the carousel show portraying 20th-century technological advances through the experiences of one Audio-Animatronics family; neon-lit Tomorrowland palm trees.*

RIGHT:
*Tongue-in-cheek signage welcomes visitors to the new Tomorrowland.*

BELOW:
*Inside the revamped Circle-Vision 360 theater, now known as the Transportarium, the robotic inventor Timekeeper (voiced by Robin Williams) and the camera-droid 9-Eye (voiced by Rhea Perlman) take the audience on a film adventure.*

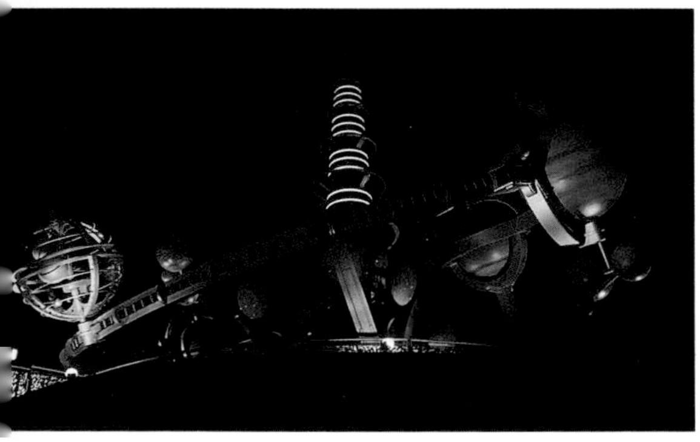

ABOVE:
*At the Astro Orbiter passengers can board Buck Rogers–style rockets for a thrilling ride.*

And so Tomorrowland stood, virtually unchanged, for nearly two decades. The cold austerity of the architecture, combined with the relentless technological messages inherent in its shows, made Tomorrowland markedly dated by the beginning of the 1990s. The sad reality was that technology was not a savior and that much of the advancement anticipated during the 1950s and 1960s had pushed people farther apart instead of bringing them together.

There was the challenge for the Imagineers: How do you present a world of tomorrow that doesn't become horribly dated by the time it's built? How do you present visions of the future whose optimism doesn't seem misguided or even sinister? The Imagineers at Disneyland Paris set their sights back 100 years, and created Discoveryland, a Tomorrowland from the point of view of 19th-century visionaries like Jules Verne and H. G. Wells. This reconception proved quite successful, and the Imagineers for Tomorrowland at Walt Disney World decided on a similar approach. They didn't go back quite so far into the past for their tomorrow; they portrayed the future as seen by early-20th-century visionaries, both real and fictional. The result is a comic science-*fantasy* community of the future, a celebration of the machine age, with tongue firmly planted in cheek. The influence of science fiction films like *Things to Come* (1936) and *Just Imagine* (1930) is evident, as is the inspiration of art styles from magazine art, like *Buck Rogers in the 25th Century, Amazing Stories,* and *Popular Science.* Reopened in 1994, the new Tomorrowland added new attractions, revamped existing ones to new themes, and re-dressed the entire visual style of Tomorrowland.

The grand promenade that leads from the central Plaza into Tomorrowland is now known as the Avenue of the Planets. Colorful and kinetic exposed structural, machine, and lighting elements carry out the science-fantasy feel, and through attention to design detail a Disney version of a dreamed community has been created. Tomorrowland is treated as a city unto itself, where humans, aliens, and robots all work together. It is the earth-site headquarters of the League of Planets and has a Chamber of Commerce, Convention Center, transit system, picture-phone service, mail service, even a newspaper, the *Tomorrowland Times.*

Existing Tomorrow-landmarks have been completely redesigned to reflect the new story being told. In place of the StarJets and their Saturn rocket pylon is Rockettower Plaza, a towering kinetic centerpiece, encircled by the Buck Rogers rockets of the Astro Orbiter. Tomorrowland Transit Authority has taken over the WEDWay PeopleMover. Beneath the Astro Orbiter is Rockettower Plaza Station, boarding point for the Metroliner Blueline, offering a comic guided tour of the Tomorrowland community and its suburbs. The proud sponsor of Take Flight (the former Dreamflight) and Walt Disney's Carousel of Progress is the Tomorrowland Metro-Retro Society.

Filmmaker George Lucas collaborated with the Imagineers on The ExtraTERRORestrial Alien Encounter, which can be found at the site of the old Mission to Mars facility. Under a massive transmission tower, the Tomorrowland Interplanetary Convention Center is the laboratory showcase of X-S Tech, a mysterious corporation from a distant planet, on a mission to impress earthlings with its line of high-tech consumer products. One of the display technologies, an interplanetary teleportation apparatus, is demonstrated to Magic Kingdom visitors and (naturally) goes terribly wrong, unleashing a fearsome alien beast in the closed auditorium. Audio-Animatronics, lighting, and other in-theater effects, combined with lifelike binaural sound, make this sensory thriller one of the most frightening ever developed by Disney.

The Circle-Vision 360 theater is now the home of The Timekeeper, based on the popular Disneyland Paris attraction known as Le Visionarium. Premiered at Disneyland Paris in 1992, Le Visionarium is the first Circle-Vision 360 attraction to incorporate Audio-Animatronics, three-dimensional animation, and special effects in the 360-degree medium. Hosted by a robotic inventor named Timekeeper and an intrepid little camera-droid known as 9-Eye, this film adventure encounters people, places, and events from the vivid tapestry of history—plus a few surprises from the future.

LIGHTS ON PARADE

One of the property's longest-running entertainment attractions is the Electrical Water Pageant on Seven Seas Lagoon and Bay Lake. Colorful creatures of the deep and mythical characters float past the hotel and Magic Kingdom shores every evening. Giant wire screens, built on 14 separate barges and supported by an intricate on-board electrical system, contain hundreds of pin lights arranged in shapes such as a dragon's head, a munching apatosaurus,

TOP:
*Within the ExtraTERRORestrial Alien Encounter, the audience encounters an unexpected visitor.*

BOTTOM:
*The entry to a display of X-S Tech's wares sets the stage for the ExtraTERRORestrial Alien Encounter.*

*A view down the Avenue of the Planets, looking toward Rockettower Plaza, in the new Tomorrowland.*

*No, it's not Loch Ness—this illuminated "monster" parades on Bay Lake and Seven Seas Lagoon as a part of the popular nightly water pageant, a staple of Walt Disney World since 1971, and the inspiration for the beloved Main Street Electrical Parade. Colorful creatures of the deep and mythical characters float past the shores of the Magic Kingdom and several resorts every evening.*

and playful dolphins. Each barge contains an on-board sound system, so that as each character appears, it has its own musical theme. At the end of the "aquacade" is a "salute to America," with flags and twinkling stars. Only canceled during high winds and inclement weather, the show has been running since October 26, 1971.

Its colorful appeal and synthesized music inspired the same show designers to create a whole new nighttime presentation, which premiered at Disneyland and was later staged for 14 seasons in the Magic Kingdom: the Main Street Electrical Parade. Floats representing many Disney icons told their stories along the parade route. There was a circus, a journey through Wonderland, Captain Hook's pirate ship, and a royal procession for Cinderella. Individual synthesized music tracks accompanied each parade unit, tied together with an overall score melody, "Baroque Hoedown." The floats themselves were small battery-powered vehicles covered in wire-mesh frames fashioned into animals, bugs, clock towers, and the like, then covered with dark or reflective cloth to hide drivers, speakers, and equipment. Thousands of tiny colored light bulbs were attached to the frames, creating sparkling illuminated illustrations of these fantasy characters.

The Main Street Electrical Parade made its Disneyland debut in 1972. The Magic Kingdom version premiered June 11, 1977, and continued until 1991. That year, as part of the Walt Disney World 20th Anniversary celebration, the intimate charm of the Main Street Electrical Parade gave way to the all-stops-pulled spectacular, SpectroMagic. (The Main Street Electrical Parade was moved to Disneyland Paris.) Although thematically similar in its presentation of iconic Disney characters and stories, SpectroMagic uses electroluminescent and fiber-optic technologies, light-spreading thermoplastics, clouds of underlit liquid nitrogen, and smoke in addition to the Electrical Parade's thousands of twinkling lights.

## CONTINUING THE DREAM

Some ideas for the resort seemed to work better on paper than they did in reality. At the Polynesian Resort there was a plan to use a wave-making machine to create artificial waves crashing along the beach. The technology appeared to

*SpectroMagic premiered in 1991 as part of the Walt Disney World 20th Anniversary celebration. To the beat of a special musical score, dozens of beloved Disney characters and stories parade down Main Street enhanced by the latest electroluminescent and fiber-optic technologies, light-spreading thermoplastics, clouds of underlit liquid nitrogen, smoke, and thousands of twinkling lights.*

work well—at one point during testing, the waves were even large enough for surfing. But the faux-surf also caused massive beach erosion, and as a result the wave machine was permanently shut down just a few months after the resort opened (its remains still lie beneath Seven Seas Lagoon). It would be 18 years before the artificial surf would again be up at Walt Disney World, at Typhoon Lagoon.

But successes far outnumbered failures in the first five years of Walt Disney World. The planned Phase One had, for the most part, reached completion. Controlled growth and expansion continued. Attendance was more than 10 million in the first year of operation, and by 1975 nearly 50 million guests had come to visit. The year 1975 was a turning point for Walt Disney World. The Disney organization continued to study the economic and creative feasibility of building Walt's ultimate dream, the display city of EPCOT. On July 14, 1975, the Disney company announced plans to proceed with an EPCOT project. However, this project would be different from the original concept that Walt Disney had envisioned. Instead of an actual working city of the future, EPCOT would be a showcase of ideas, a place for people to come and learn about themselves and the world around them, through the use of Disney technology and entertainment.

# CHAPTER FOUR
# EPCOT

*The only problem with anything "of tomorrow" is that at the pace we're going right now, tomorrow would catch up with us before we got it built.*

—WALT DISNEY

*Walt Disney stands proudly before a site plan of the proposed central city of his Florida project, known as EPCOT—Experimental Prototype Community of Tomorrow.*

OPPOSITE:
*Spaceship Earth at night.*

That quote from Walt Disney succinctly describes the path of his EPCOT dream. Walt's original concept for EPCOT was exactly what the acronym describes: an Experimental Prototype Community of Tomorrow, a genuine laboratory of urban development where people would live, work, and play, testing the newest technological advances available. Much as the measure of previous civilizations has been in artistic, spiritual, or military advances, Walt believed technology would enable us to improve as a society.

Walt's utopian fantasy was probably an unachievable goal. Time and again, the model city concept has failed because controlling and legislating the behavior of the population have proven impossible. Today, this new city concept seems like the stuff of optimistic—but impractical—science fiction.

Walt's creative heirs, continually being judged by the media and the public, suffered a great dilemma. They could carry forth with an urban development project of gargantuan proportions (a project that faced the very real possibility of conceptual failure, corporate embarrassment, and a complete drain on the company's funds) or face the slings and arrows that would come with their perceived failure to carry out Walt's last great dream. In the end, compromise was inevitable, and the solution was relatively simple: the concepts and ideals embodied in Walt's best intentions for his model city could be folded into a new take on one of Disney's great strengths—the theme park. The best explanation of this shift in execution comes from the official program for the Grand Opening and Dedication Ceremony of EPCOT Center (1982):

> *Some twenty years ago, long before the opening of Walt Disney World, Walt Disney envisioned a place where the greatest feats of human imagination and invention could be communicated to the benefit of all people. He called his idea "EPCOT"—the Experimental Prototype Community of Tomorrow—for he wanted to present alternatives and possibilities for a better life ahead.*

*Walt Disney's death on December 15, 1966, was a critical event for the company. His vision of "a new Disney World" outside Orlando, Florida, especially his concept of EPCOT, was so strongly a personal, life-summing statement that many believed the dream might die with Walt. Not so. For in addition to the fantasy empire he had created, he had also built a unique organization . . . determined to carry out the plan Walt had outlined. . . . When, in July 1975, Walt Disney Productions announced it was moving forward with plans for EPCOT, to some it was a bolt of lightning. . . .*

*From the beginning, Walt Disney World has been planned, constructed and developed with EPCOT concepts in mind. Futuristic designs and technologies have been put into action as a matter of policy—monorail and linear induction power transportation systems, a solar-powered office building, state-of-the-art waste treatment processes, the first all-electronic, fiber-optics telephone system, and much more. Since 1971, Walt Disney World has been host to the world—130 million people from 100 nations have visited this community.*

*The planners, designers, engineers, and operators of Walt Disney World are already providing nearly all the public services of a city, from communications and security to waste disposal. Implemented by the Reedy Creek Improvement District, the EPCOT Building Code, embodying Walt's philosophy for EPCOT, is firmly in place as the foundation for future development. What was lacking was a public focus for new ideas and concepts, a "center" for the communication of new possibilities for the future—directly to the public.*

*To answer this need, we are developing EPCOT Center: a permanent World's Fair of imagination, discovery, education and exploration that combines the Disney entertainment and communications skills with the knowledge and predictions for the future of authorities from industry, the academic world, and the professions. Our goal is to inspire the visitors who come here, so that they will be turned on to the positive potential of the future and will want to participate in making the choices that shape it. We believe that in a world where cynicism and negativism abound, there is another story, and we have chosen, with forethought and conviction, to tell it, and to be that voice of optimism.*

*Now we have a way to bring real focus to the import of creative and futuristic processes and the value of friendship among nations. EPCOT Center is a permanent World's Fair of imagination, discovery, education, and exploration built with the help of leading American and international industries and with the cooperation of a number of governments.*

In this way, not only did the company publicly portray the entire Walt Disney World resort *as* EPCOT, but it also specifically added the exposition theme park to display the technological innovation at work in Walt Disney World.

## PROTOTYPE SYSTEMS AND ADVANCED TECHNOLOGIES AT WALT DISNEY WORLD

In a report from Walt Disney World shortly after its opening, journalist David Brinkley observed, "It is the most imaginative and effective piece of urban planning in America, and that is totally aside from the . . . amusement park area itself. It is outside the park, on Disney's own land, which is about twice the size of Manhattan. On this they built roads, transportation systems, lakes, golf courses, campgrounds, riding stables, stores, hotels, and so on. And they all fit together better than any other urban environment in America."

The oft-made comparison between Walt Disney World and a new city is not mere hyperbole. Behind the glamour of the show business is the serious business of hosting a transient community of 40,000 or so overnight guests every day.

Supporting facilities include 43 miles of winding drainage canals with innovative flood-control gates; nine acres of underground utility corridors called utilidors, an urban basement providing out-of-sight access to infrastructural services (sewer lines, pipes, cables, and garbage disposal); technical innovations such as America's first fiber-optic telephone system; the introduction in the United States of the Swedish AVAC trash-disposal system, with trash funneled underground in pneumatic tubes to a central collection point; and many other behind-the-scenes systems and services.

The prototype systems and technologies supporting the entire resort property, as well as progressive building codes, demonstration and prototype projects, and the highest environmental standards governing its development, have established Walt Disney World as an archetype in land development. Many organizations, from the International Chamber of Commerce, which met there in 1978, to the Urban Land Institute, have recognized this "living laboratory." In 1981 Walt Disney World was selected from among 200 projects to receive the Urban Land Institute Award for Excellence. This annual award, which is presented to only one national project each year, recognizes innovative land developments that embody superior design, relevance to contemporary issues and needs, and resourceful utilization of land while improving the quality of the living environment.

*World Showcase from the courtyard level in a concept painting by Herbert Ryman.*

THE ORIGINS OF EPCOT CENTER

EPCOT Center can trace its roots directly to the Disney attractions at the 1964–65 New York World's Fair. Indeed, it repeats much of the thematic litany of the fair: a utopian faith in progress through technological development. The resulting park is often described as a permanent world's fair, for it takes not only its thematic approach from such expositions, but its physical design cues as well.

The first announcement that Disney would proceed with its new take on EPCOT was made in May of 1974 by then-president and chief operating officer of Walt Disney Productions E. Cardon ("Card") Walker.

"In a real sense, the concept for EPCOT has been unfolding from the very beginning," Walker said. "From the outset of planning and through the design, construction and installation stages of Walt Disney World, EPCOT has been the ultimate goal."

"It seems to me that we will begin [the EPCOT project] with the construction of a permanent international showcase, in which the nations of the world may participate on a permanent basis to demonstrate their culture and

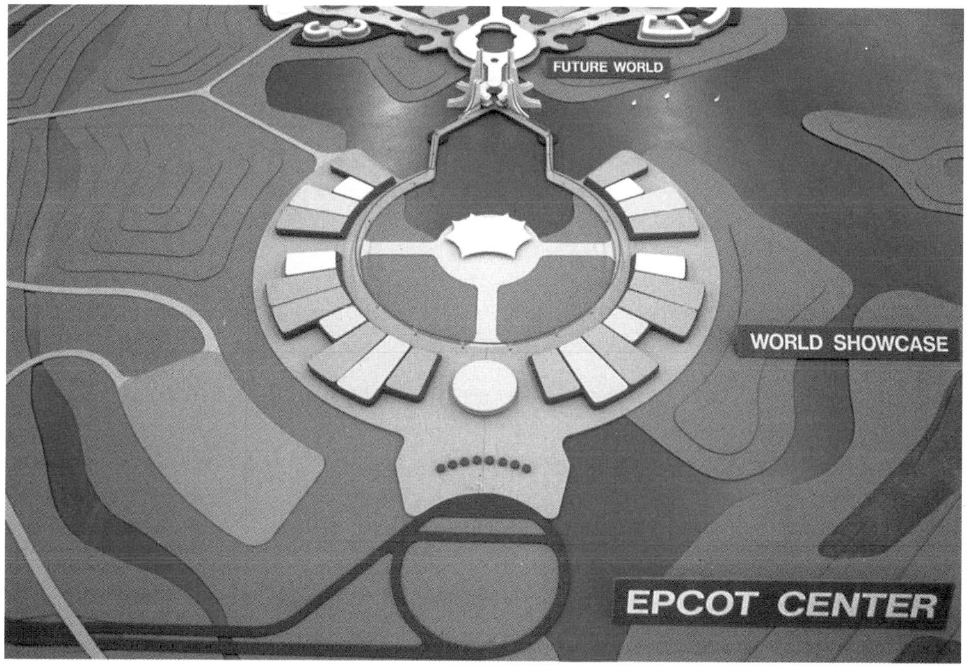


*An early site model for EPCOT Center with World Showcase as the entry component. The initial intent was that World Showcase would serve as an enticement to guests and that the "topic" pavilions of Future World, added later, would be ancillary.*

their products," Walker added. This was the first announcement of the concept behind the World Showcase half of EPCOT Center. For the next few years, it was assumed that World Showcase would be the primary and initial component of the project to be constructed. Future World, the futurist environment and technology exhibit area, was as yet undefined.

Walker then outlined seven specific objectives to serve as a starting point for further discussion and advancement of "the EPCOT concept":

1. *To encourage industry and the professions to introduce, test, and demonstrate new ideas, materials, and systems.*
2. *To showcase and prove the usefulness of promising concepts, technology, and specific prototype products.*
3. *To provide an ongoing "meeting place" where creative people of science, industry, and the arts from around the world may gather for days or weeks or months to discuss and develop specific solutions to the specific needs of mankind.*
4. *To advance the excellence of environmental planning.*
5. *To bring together, in a living, working, creative environment, people of varied interests, talents, and backgrounds who will live together for days or weeks or months in a community and climate where experimentation is accepted and fundamental.*
6. *To create an artful and efficient environment—a community fashioned in human terms and human scale that begins with the belief that the people who live and work and play in it are the heart of the city.*
7. *To provide, for the first time anywhere, a practical basis for investigating and proving not only the "popularity"—but also the economic feasibility of new ideas, materials, and systems introduced and tested here.*

The initial master plan, focusing on World Showcase, was presented in July 1975, in a ceremony at the Contemporary Resort, with invited dignitaries from Australia, Denmark, Germany, Greece, Italy, Mexico, Israel, the USSR, the Philippines, Romania, the United Kingdom, Venezuela, Belgium, New Zealand, and Iran in attendance.

The World Showcase unveiled at this meeting bears a strong conceptual resemblance to the World Showcase as built, but the physical differences are quite startling. Initially World Showcase was envisioned as a gigantic semicircular building with all the pavilions contained *within* the building itself. Along the interior crescent, each nation's pavilion entrance would contain the same amount of street frontage, regardless of how much space the pavilion contained behind the facade. The intent of the design was to alleviate visual competition or any perception that the most impressive facade contained the most impressive attractions.

What would become Future World was described in this initial presentation as the EPCOT Theme Center. "The EPCOT Center will be a central core or plaza where visitors will be introduced to the multiple ideas and

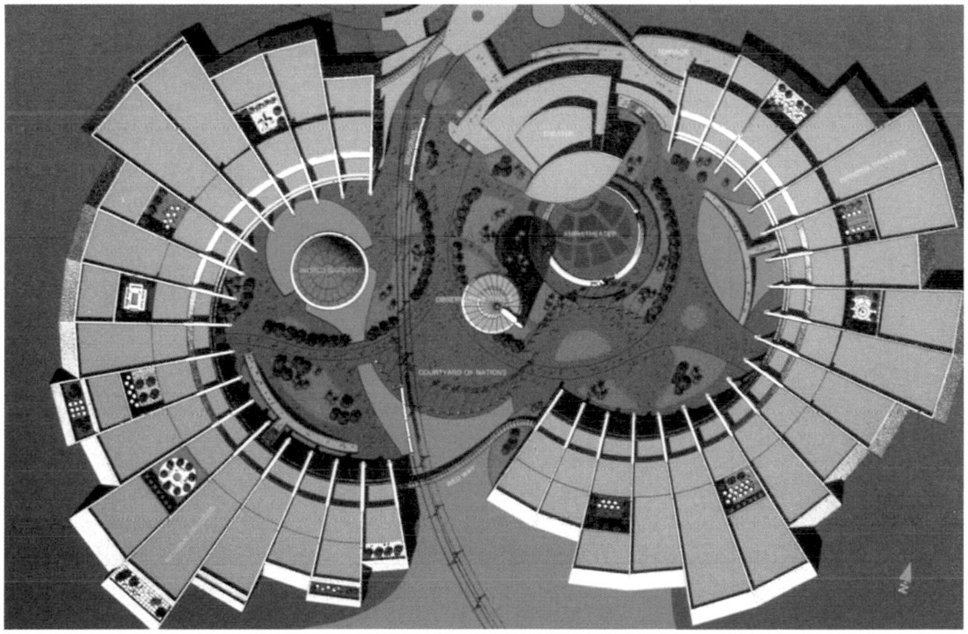

ABOVE:
*Concept painting of one of the early design approaches to World Showcase, showing it as two connected semicircular structures containing all the national pavilions.*

LEFT:
*The same concept viewed as a site footprint with its Courtyard of Nations, high-rise Observation Tower, and 30 pavilions. Although the pavilions differed in square footage, they all had the same amount of frontage along the interior courtyard.*

concepts of EPCOT," the overview stated. This was the first use of the name "EPCOT Center." After entering the theme center, visitors could choose three pavilions, focusing on the major issues of science and technology, communication and the arts, and community. Guests could then move on to satellite pavilions that would represent the latest research and development in medicine, agriculture, transportation, energy, education, or international relations.

The initial EPCOT plan was that World Showcase, with its "Courtyard of Nations," high-rise Observation Tower, and 30 pavilions, would be the main draw. The pavilions of the EPCOT Theme Center, to be added later, were planned as ancillary. After two years and a discouraging response from foreign sponsors to the World Showcase project, it was decided that the project's second phase, now called Future World, would be built simultaneously. In that way, funding from corporations participating in Future World would be available from the outset to finance the entire project.

In Glendale, the Imagineers geared up for the greatest challenge in the history of their creative group. The core team of Imagineers included Carl Borgirno, president of administration and finance; Marty Sklar, executive vice president of creative development; John Hench, senior vice president of design; Don Edgren, vice president of engineering; and Randy Bright, vice president of concepts. Hundreds of scientific and historical experts were consulted to ensure consistent detail and technological accuracy. The various films in each attraction required more than 16 production crews to produce. With new, improved fiber optics, lasers, computers, water controls, and digital sound (a premier technology at the time) the park was to have five times the number of special effects in the Magic Kingdom. In the end, more than 200 new special effects were developed (Journey Into Imagination alone had 78).

Imagineering teams traveled to the foreign countries participating in World Showcase. They studied the history, culture, and world contributions of each nation, then based the theme of each showcase on historical and architectural landmarks of recognizable cities. Many of the Imagineers who had planned, designed, and supervised the creation of the Magic Kingdom worked on this project. Now, instead of constructing pirates and flying elephants, their task was to create dinosaurs and space colonies, advanced greenhouses and marine habitats. The experiences in EPCOT Center had to be the closest visitors could come to the real thing—past, present, or future.

By the time the EPCOT project was completed, the WED staff had increased from 450 to 2,500, housed in every available space that could be found in their Glendale offices, at the Walt Disney Studios in neighboring Burbank, in an assembly plant in North Hollywood, at Disneyland, and even on a sound stage at the 20th Century-Fox Studio in West Los Angeles.

## STAKING OUT THE TERRITORY

The location chosen for EPCOT Center was a 550-acre site about two and a half miles south of the Magic Kingdom, almost directly in the center of the Walt Disney World property. The locale had been identified by Walt Disney as the desired site for the downtown core of the futuristic city he planned.

The postshow area of TheWalt Disney Story on Main Street, U.S.A. in the Magic Kingdom became the EPCOT Preview Center. Here, visitors could become acquainted with the new park and its conceptual underpinnings through a film, elaborate models, and concept artwork. When the

The "official" concept painting of EPCOT Center.

monorail track extension to EPCOT Center was completed, trains took visitors to the site for a view of the construction in progress.

Construction began in October 1979. The gargantuan scale of the project made it the largest private construction project in the world. The budget was set at a staggering $600 million, but by the end of the project it was estimated that Disney had spent anywhere between $800 million and $1.2 billion. WED Enterprises, Walt Disney World Co., Buena Vista Construction Company, and Tishman Construction Corporation supervised the more than 10,000 workers who were ultimately involved in bringing EPCOT Center to life.

The concept of EPCOT Center was so new it was treated as its own organic, self-contained culture, with no relationship to the Magic Kingdom or other Disney products. No costumed Disney characters greeted guests at EPCOT Center; there was no Disney character merchandise in any of the shops; and since the intended audience for the park was older than that of the Magic Kingdom, the World Showcase pavilions were allowed to serve alcohol. A few years later the EPCOT name was just as Disney-identified in the visitors' mind as the Disney label, so Disney characters appeared both in the park and in the shops.

### GRAND OPENING

October 1, 1982, was the beginning of opening month for EPCOT Center, with the EPCOT Center Grand Opening and Dedication Ceremony taking place on Sunday, October 24. The 11:00 A.M. event started with a fanfare of trumpets, a dedication hymn by the West Point Glee Club, performances by the All-American College Marching Band, the International Ceremony of the Waters (a symbolic blending of water from across the globe, in the fountain behind Spaceship Earth), and a precision flyover by the Florida Air National Guard. Read by Card Walker, the dedication plaque proclaimed:

> *To all who come to this Place of Joy, Hope and Friendship, Welcome. EPCOT is inspired by Walt Disney's creative vision. Here, human achievements are celebrated through imagination, wonders of enterprise and concepts of a future that promises new and exciting benefits for all. May EPCOT Center entertain, inform and inspire and, above all, may it instill a new sense of belief and pride in man's ability to shape a world that offers hope to people everywhere.*

### THE CENTERPIECE: SPACESHIP EARTH

The basic layout of EPCOT Center is an hourglass shape, each circular end containing a major theme area. To the north are the Future World pavilions, dedicated to such issues as communications, energy, health, technological futurism, transportation, imagination, the land, and the sea. These pavilions are arranged around the theme icon—a huge geodesic sphere, Spaceship Earth, presented by AT&T. On a 1.3-mile strand around a 40-acre lagoon at the south end is World Showcase, a curving line of microcosmic countries: Mexico, Norway, China, Germany, Italy, the United States, Japan, Morocco, France, the United Kingdom, and Canada. Most of these pavilions feature a show, film, or attraction; restaurants; shops; and tourist information.

*Aerial view of EPCOT Center under construction, showing the monorail, the FutureWorld pavilions around the geodesic sphere of Spaceship Earth, and the World Showcase pavilions along the lagoon.*

The EPCOT Center landmark, Spaceship Earth, took 26 months to build. As the symbol of the park and its statement of world understanding, it required a distinctive design, so the world's first geodesic sphere was created. It is 180 feet high and 165 feet in diameter, with an estimated weight of 16 million pounds. About 1,700 tons of steel were used to build the sphere. Support pilings for its six pylon legs are buried from 120 to 185 feet deep. The sphere is actually composed of two spheres, one inside the other. The inner sphere contains the track and rooms of the attraction, as well as maintenance areas. The outer sphere is held about two feet away from the inner sphere by aluminum hubs. A special type of aluminum called alucobond, consisting of two anodized aluminum faces and a polyethylene core, was used for the 11,324 silvered facets on 954 triangular panels covering the globe. This material can withstand the Florida climate and is self-cleaning. A specially developed gutter system prevents rain from cascading off the sphere; rainwater is channeled through the structure and sent to underground drains, where it replenishes the World Showcase Lagoon.

The attraction within the giant sphere traces the story of human communication, from Cro-Magnon man to ancient Egypt, Phoenicia, and Greece, Rome, Gutenberg's Germany, and Renaissance Italy, all the way to the radio days of the 1930s and 1940s, and right up to today. The 15-minute ride-through Audio-Animatronics spectacular was assembled with the consultation of futurist and author Ray Bradbury, the Smithsonian Institution, the Huntington Library, the University of Southern California, and the University of Chicago. The show itself is rife with detail, from the replica Gutenberg Bible to the graffiti reproduced from the walls of Pompeii. At the exit area of Spaceship Earth, the latest communication technology is on display in Global Neighborhood.

TOP LEFT AND RIGHT:
*The largest geodesic sphere of its kind to "float" off the ground, Spaceship Earth is 180 feet high and 165 feet in diameter.*

ABOVE:
*The attraction within Spaceship Earth traces the history of communication, including prehistoric cave drawings and storytelling* (TOP) *and the art of Renaissance Italy* (BOTTOM).

## INNOVENTIONS

Beyond Spaceship Earth the central semicircular structures were originally Communicore East and Communicore West. The Communicores contained specific exhibits and demonstrations in a hands-on atmosphere of exploration and fun.

In 1994 Communicore was redesigned and renamed Innoventions, an all-new collection of interactive displays and demonstrations. Rather than dealing with far-flung futurism, Innoventions focuses on a future that's just around the corner, in exhibits hosted by the cutting-edge technology companies of today. The information superhighway, advanced computer software, digital television, virtual reality, voice-controlled appliances, electric cars, and smart-house features are the stuff of Innoventions. Visitors to Innoventions have the opportunity to play the newest video games, try out state-of-the-art personal computer technologies, and experience the home of tomorrow. Although products are not sold in exhibit areas, representatives from each exhibiting company are on hand to explain and demonstrate the products on display. Guests may use interactive computer terminals to receive information by mail.

The monochrome institutional look of Communicore gave way to bold, bright colors, lively graphics, and kinetic elements. (Much of this new visual approach was the work of longtime Imagineer Rolly Crump, who created the Tower of the Four Winds for the 1964–65 New York World's Fair and the initial design of the DNA tower at Wonders of Life.) The Stargate and Sunrise Terrace restaurants were replaced by new eateries, including the Electric Umbrella restaurant, Pasta Piazza Ristorante, and Fountain View Espresso & Bakery.

The Innoventions concept is established in a multimedia show hosted in typical fashion by popular television personality Bill Nye, the Science

*At Innoventions visitors can discover and even try out the very latest technological advances, from new computer software to controlled appliances to electric cars. Bright colors, lively graphics and kinetic elements all add to the excitement of this look into the immediate future.*

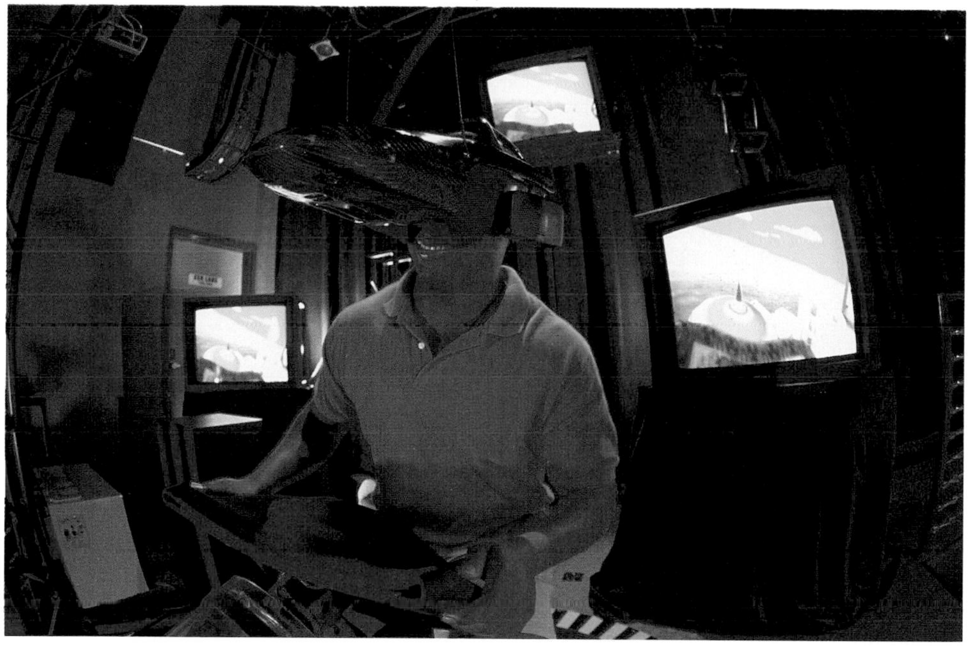

*The first demonstration at the Walt Disney Imagineering Laboratory at Innoventions was for Aladdin's Magic Carpet. Through a state-of-the-art imaging system combining animation art and virtual reality, selected Epcot guests could "try out" the flying carpet adventure while other guests watched.*

Guy. His demonstrations include a television screen that bulges to follow the contours of a human face.

An initial Innoventions highlight was the Walt Disney Imagineering Laboratory (temporarily closed). For the first time, guests can go inside a Disney lab to see experimentation on a future theme park attraction during development. The premiere demonstration, for Aladdin's Magic Carpet, used a super-power computer-graphic imaging system combining Disney animation art with virtual reality. The audience was able to watch the VR lab as it tested the flying carpet experience with selected Epcot guests.

Innoventions also houses the Epcot Discovery Center, a resource supplying further information, discussion guides, and direction to ancillary resources to educators and visitors interested in the myriad topics in and questions raised by Epcot exhibits. In addition, the staff is well versed in Disney history and Walt Disney World lore and attempts to answer any lingering trivia questions about all subjects Disney. The largest merchandise location at Epcot, the Centorium, is also in the Innoventions facility.

UNIVERSE OF ENERGY

On the southwest side of Spaceship Earth is a distinctive wedge-shaped building (even the southern live oaks to one side of the pavilion entrance are pruned to mimic its shape). This reflective, telescoping structure houses the Universe of Energy, sponsored by Exxon. Its roof is covered with two acres of photovoltaic cells, which convert sunlight directly into electrical energy, providing 15 percent of the power required to run the attraction inside.

When EPCOT opened, the Universe of Energy featured a film presentation examining the different types of energy being used today. The projection surface is composed of 100 solid triangular elements that rotate on

TOP: *The building for the Universe of Energy is an unusual wedge shape.* CENTER: *Its roof is covered with two acres of photovoltaic cells, which convert sunlight into some of the electrical energy used to run the attraction inside.* BOTTOM: *As part of the presentation on the origin of fossil fuel, visitors travel through a three-dimensional Audio-Animatronics version of the primeval world.*

computer cue in synchronization with the changing projected images, to create a kinetic visual mosaic. In the adjoining area, visitors are seated for a second film, which was an animated short depicting the origins of fossil fuels. At the conclusion of the film, the entire seating area rotates and breaks up into six vehicle-sections that begin to move through a three-dimensional Audio-Animatronics re-creation of the primeval world. After exploring prehistory, the vehicles reassemble into a theater again, where a finale motion picture is shown on an immense, enveloping 220-degree screen (the angle of view of human vision is 165 degrees by 60 degrees).

Initially, the Imagineers were extremely circumspect in their presentation of relevant and scientific information. In many cases, the desire for credibility made some of the presentations seem diffident, staid, even dull. With the opening of Wonders of Life in 1989, a new, more relaxed presentation style made its debut. While the information presented is no less authoritative, the Imagineers no longer hesitate to showcase presentations that are satiric, comic, and fun—frequently involving television and movie stars and other celebrities.

The 1996 version of the Universe of Energy show, for example, has become "Ellen's Energy Crisis," starring television comedian Ellen DeGeneres. Ellen falls asleep and dreams that she is in competition on *Jeopardy!*™ with her college rival (Jamie Lee Curtis), where all the categories relate to energy. Thanks to her next-door neighbor (Bill Nye, the Science Guy), Ellen (with the group of Epcot guests) embarks on a journey through the past, present, and future to learn about energy—and make a dazzling comeback in Final Jeopardy! Also featured in this new presentation are Wallace Shawn, Alex Trebek, Tim Conway, Rue McClanahan, and John Ratzenberger.

### WONDERS OF LIFE

Although on the EPCOT Center drawing boards since 1975, the so-called Life and Health pavilion didn't find a corporate patron until MetLife came on board in 1986. The pavilion itself is a 100,000-square-foot gold geodesic dome, inside which visitors find a large, bright, airy interconnection of attractions, the Fitness Fairgrounds. The light, color, and kineticism of the domed interior give the place a festive courtyard atmosphere.

At Met Lifestyle Revue, visitors enter basic data at an interactive computer terminal and are given advice about how to improve their health. With Wonder Cycles, computerized stationary bicycles with video monitors, riders can "bicycle" through locales including the Tournament of Roses Parade and Disneyland. At Coach's Corner, pro athletes offer advice on visitors' golf, tennis, and baseball swings via computer analysis and laser disc playback. The Sensory Funhouse has hands-on activities pertaining to sight (optical illusions abound), touch, and sound.

Off the central path is a little open theater with a cartoon cityscape, on which the drama *Goofy About Health* is enacted. Using several vintage

Goofy cartoons as well as new animation, this clever show portrays the character's transformation from slob to super-goof. Nearby, at the Anacomical Players Theater, an improvisation group presents a live show about health and fitness issues. A third theater shows the 14-minute film *The Making of Me*, a remarkable and sensitive portrayal of conception and childbirth, starring Martin Short and directed by Glen Gordon Caron.

Cranium Command is a delightfully Disney kind of show, with just the right balance of humor, technology, and information. The 17-minute show begins with an animated film in which General Knowledge recruits pilots for a new assignment, into people's brains. Buzzy is assigned to a 12-year-old boy. As visitors enter the theater, they realize they are seated *inside* the boy's head. Buzzy pilots the audience through the boy's typical morning, with the help of the left brain (Charles Grodin), the right brain (Jon Lovitz),

ABOVE LEFT:
*The entry to Wonders of Life is dominated by the Tower of Life, a 76-foot, 25-ton double-helix tower based upon the molecular structure of DNA.*

ABOVE RIGHT:
*The pavilion itself is housed under a golden geodesic dome, a frame of interlocking tetrahedral shapes copied from the natural structure of crystals and plant cells.*

the stomach (George Wendt), the adrenal gland (Bobcat Goldthwait), and the heart (Dana Carvey and Kevin Nealon).

The Imagineers had struggled over the years with a presentation method for one of the pavilion's key attractions. The intent was to send a vehicle of visitors on a microscopic journey through the human body, much as in the 1966 science fiction film *Fantastic Voyage.* However, the full-scale mechanical effects required to open and close a 30-foot heart valve and inflate and deflate 8-foot alveoli simply didn't work. It wasn't until the simulator technology of Star Tours proved effective in 1986 that this human body attraction, called Body Wars, was put back into development. Instead of being presented full size in dimensional sets, the microscopic views of blood vessels and organs are created on film. The 44 passengers inside the simulator vehicle are sent on a "routine" medical probe—from the inside. Naturally, as when anything is labeled just "routine," things go wrong, and the vehicle (and its passengers) must rush through the body at bumpy, breakneck speed.

Frontiers of Medicine is the one area in Wonders of Life *without* tongue in cheek. Here, a variety of scientific and educational exhibits reveal the cutting edge of medical research and technology—and it's not nearly as boring as it might sound.

### HORIZONS

North of Wonders of Life is the monumental gold wedge Horizons—it has the look of a spacecraft that has set down on the site. Horizons opened on October 1, 1983. The pavilion was developed under the working name "Century 3" (a reflection of the United States entering the third century of its existence).

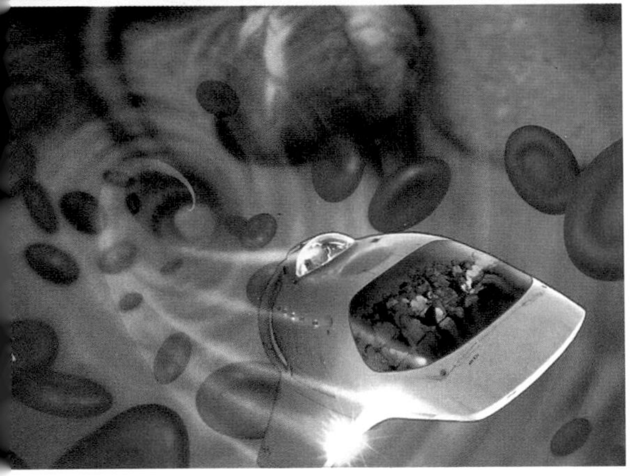

ABOVE: *In Cranium Command* (TOP), *Buzzy steers the audience through a 12-year-old boy's typical morning. In Body Wars* (BOTTOM), *44 passengers inside a simulator vehicle whizz through the inside of a human body.*

RIGHT: *The large gold wedge of Horizons looks like a spacecraft that has just landed.*

LEFT: *Inside Horizons, visitors traveled through Audio-Animatronics tableaux about futurism.*

BELOW: *World of Motion featured a comic account of transportation history from animal power to airplanes. The graceful, reflective exterior of the circular pavilion* (BOTTOM LEFT) *resembles a sublime interpretation of an automotive air filter or machine component.*

More than any of the Future World pavilions, Horizons was explicitly about futurism. Visitors seated in unique suspended four-passenger vehicles traveled through Audio-Animatronics tableaux, such as "Looking Back at Tomorrow," a review of past visions of the future. Next, in the Omnisphere theater, the vehicles passed a pair of 80-foot hemispherical screens displaying a Space Shuttle launch, growing crystals, and animated scenes of a space colony—all an introduction to a series of tableaux depicting life in the future, in Nova Cite (an urban center in Space), Mesa Verde (a desert farming community), and Sea Castle (an underwater city). Finally, visitors could choose one of three "endings," based on a vote by the majority of vehicle passengers. Horizons exhibited much of the technology-based optimistic futurism of another favorite show, Carousel of Progress.

Since 1993, Horizons has fluctuated between being open and closed, but it is slated to be replaced by a new pavilion in the future—possibly a pavilion on Space.

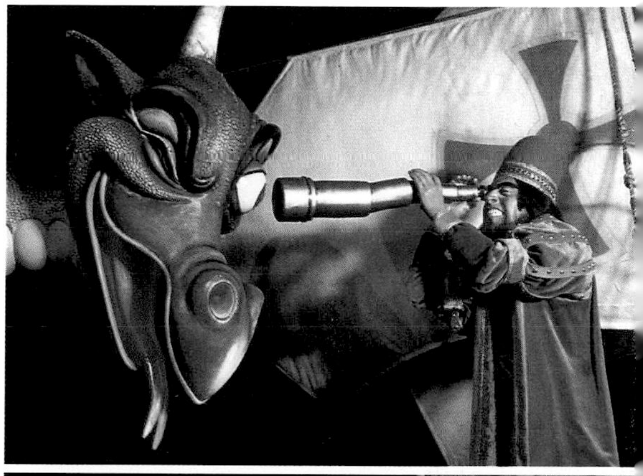

## WORLD OF MOTION

The circular World of Motion, sponsored by General Motors, is the next pavilion in the Future World chain. The original ride-through show in the World of Motion resembled Pirates of the Caribbean in its presentation style (although it had been planned as a film-based show), a comic telling of the history of manned transportation. Many of the gags used were the brainchild of legendary Disney artist Ward Kimball, who had animated Jiminy Cricket in *Pinocchio* (1940) and won an Academy Award for the short *It's Tough to Be a Bird* (1969). A confirmed eccentric, Kimball supervised the entire series of farcical Audio-Animatronics tableaux, depicting vehicles from animal power to internal combustion.

In 1997 the World of Motion will be completely replaced by a new General Motors thrill "show," modeled after a GM test track. Visitors will get a behind-the-scenes glimpse into the world of proving (and *im*proving) automobiles and will actually experience a test drive on a simulated variable speed, multisurface, multi-environment test track—traveling at speeds of up to 65 miles per hour.

## JOURNEY INTO IMAGINATION

The sparkling crystalline structure of Journey Into Imagination, presented by Kodak, glistens to the east of World of Motion. The pavilion's four-acre site includes two towering pyramids (made of triangles of mirrored glass over a tubed aluminum frame) and a picture garden full of lush landscape and fantastic fountains.

The Journey Into Imagination ride itself is a whimsical 14-minute presentation about how the human imagination works. Beginning in the Dreamport, where the senses are constantly sending data, visitors see imagination deployed into visual and performing arts, literature, and science and technology. The key characters of the ride and pavilion are Dreamfinder (a jovial, bearded, redheaded professorial fellow with the voice of comic actor Chuck McCann) and the dragonlike Figment, created with a lizard's body, a crocodile's nose, a steer's horns, two big yellow eyes, two small wings, and a pinch of childish delight (and the voice of Billy Barty).

The Magic Eye Theater opened with the film *Magic Journeys*, which used a new 65mm 3-D process developed by WED Enterprises and Eastman Kodak. On September 12, 1986, *Captain EO* premiered at the Magic Eye. This 17-minute science fantasy film starred Michael Jackson and Anjelica Huston and was produced by George Lucas and directed by Francis Ford Coppola. *Captain EO* was replaced on November 24, 1994, by an all-new 3-D film based on the Disney hits *Honey, I Shrunk the Kids* and *Honey, I Blew Up the Kid.* In *Honey, I Shrunk the Audience*, spectators enter crackpot professor Wayne Szalinski's Imagination Institute, where they become unwitting accidental victims of the professor's (in)famous shrinking ray.

*In* Honey, I Shrunk the Audience, *spectators find their whole perspective changing under a crazy professor's shrinking ray.*

OPPOSITE:
*Two different views of Journey Into Imagination, with its two towering pyramids of mirrored glass over a tubed aluminum frame.*

RIGHT:
*The Sunshine Season Food Fair inside The Land.*

BELOW:
*In Living with the Land* (TOP), *visitors travel in a boat through tropical swamps and other lands in a presentation of the difficulties of maintaining ecological balance while cultivating the land. Kitchen Kabaret* (BOTTOM) *was an early Audio-Animatronics theater show about the basic food groups.*

The pavilion's other popular attractions are Image Works, a truly ambitious interactive activity center (many visitors spend hours inside), and the famous leapfrog fountains in front of the building, which send out smooth, disconnected arcs of water from one garden plot to another.

THE LAND

South of Journey Into Imagination is The Land, presented by Nestlé. The pavilion opened in October 1982, but just over 10 years later, beginning in November of 1992, it underwent a series of extensive renovations by Walt Disney Imagineering.

Originally, in Listen to the Land a boat traveled along a water flume through tropical swamps, prairie fields, and a family farm, in a story of the struggle to maintain ecological balance while cultivating the land. The updated and renovated ride, including a new opening storm scene, is called Living with the Land and opened in December 1993.

Kitchen Kabaret was a lively Audio-Animatronics theater show about the basic four food groups, but much as the basic food groups have been superseded by the nutritional pyramid, Food Rocks replaced Kitchen Kabaret on March 26, 1994. The show now is a 15-minute mock rock concert featuring such "food groups" as the Peach Boys, Chubby Cheddar, and Pita Gabriel. Prior to the show, visitors can learn about nutrition and food through various interactive games and displays.

The Harvest Theater was home to the film *Symbiosis* from October 1982 until January 21, 1995, when it was replaced by the all-new 13-minute film *Circle of Life: An Environmental Fable.* Featuring Simba, Timon, and Pumbaa, stars of Disney's animated blockbuster *The Lion King,* this film tells a tale of environmental responsibility.

# FLOWER POWER: THE PROTOTYPE WATER HYACINTH PURIFICATION PROJECT

If ever there was an archetypal EPCOT project, the Water Hyacinth Project at Walt Disney World's Community Waste Research Center was it. In this 10-year pioneering experimental research program, which occupied a small corner of Walt Disney World's 27,000-plus acres, flowering plants—water hyacinths—turned sewage into energy and garnered worldwide recognition in the scientific community.

The project began in 1978, when it was proposed by WED Enterprises to the United States Environmental Protection Agency. Next, NASA expressed interest and, along with other organizations, contributed financial and technical assistance.

The project facility was composed of five quarter-acre rectangular ponds. The water hyacinths' large glossy green leaves and violet blossoms floated on the ponds' surfaces like lily pads. A portion of Walt Disney World's waste water flowed through the project's ponds, where the aquatic plants gorged themselves in a continual feeding frenzy. This process eliminated pollutants from 55,000 gallons of the resort's waste water each day. Additional experiments proved the hyacinth system could also treat some types of hazardous waste. As the plants became fully gorged, they were harvested and replaced with hungry ones. Cranelike rakes scooped up a ton and a half of wet hyacinths from the ponds each day. The byproduct was initially composted and used as fertilizer.

Then, in 1983, the Gas Research Institute joined the Water Hyacinth Project, introducing a method of converting the harvested hyacinths into pipeline-quality methane gas. The plants were chopped, mixed with sludge, and pumped into a huge digester vat, where the mixture underwent bioconversion.

Besides methane, further research developed other beneficial products from the hyacinths. Chemical modification of the hyacinth fiber yielded paper, particleboard, wood board, and fully biodegradable absorbent material used for disposable rags.

The water hyacinths are still used to purify water at Walt Disney World. Also, the San Diego, California, Water Utilities Department implemented a million-gallon-a-day pilot plant, which handles sewage treatment for more than two million area residents, and communities in Austin, Texas, and Orlando, Florida have implemented similar plants—all of these systems used the EPCOT Water Hyacinth Project data to establish their design criteria.

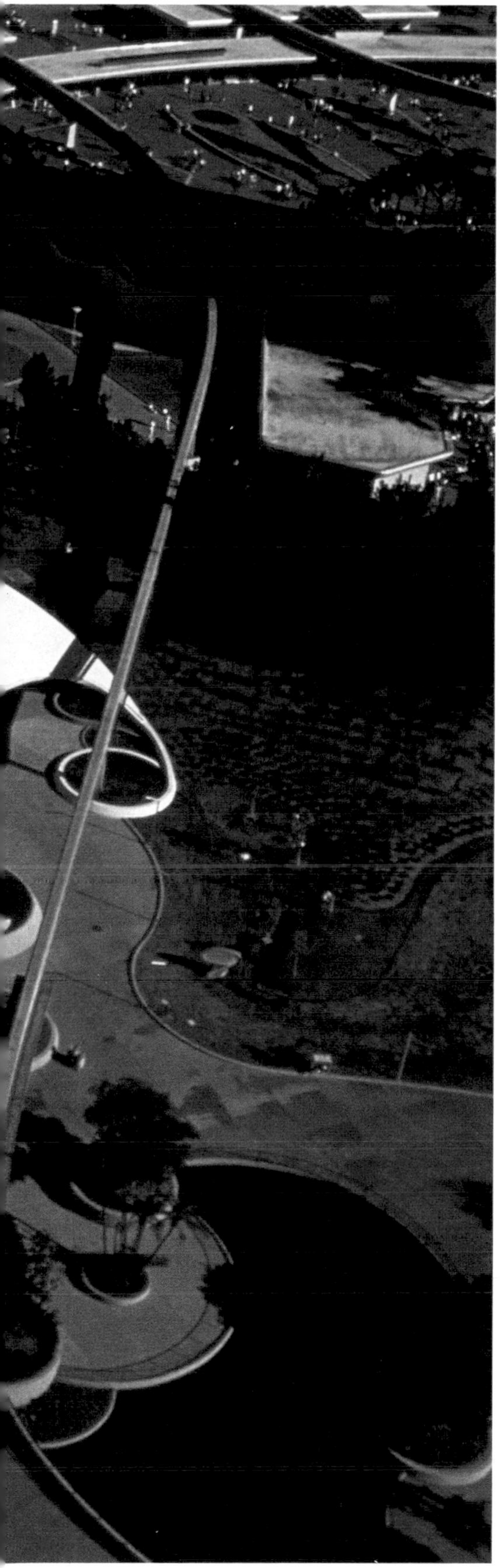

## THE LIVING SEAS

Like Horizons and Wonders of Life, The Living Seas, originally presented by United Technologies, opened after the rest of the Future World pavilions, on January 15, 1986. At the entrance is one of the most fascinating, yet simple, pavilion marquees, a rock-work "coastline" complete with crashing waves and tidal pools.

Inside, visitors can join humankind's quest to learn about the mysteries of the sea. There is a 125-foot-long sea mural, a display area that includes photos of John Lethbridge's diving barrel and Frederic de Drieberg's 1809 breathing device, as well as a diving suit and model of the submarine *Nautilus* actually used in the making of Disney's 1954 science fiction classic *20,000 Leagues Under the Sea.* A two-minute multimedia presentation honors the pioneers of ocean research, and a seven-minute special-effects film demonstrates the critical role of the sea as a source of energy, minerals, and protein. There is a ride through a Caribbean coral reef, housed in the largest saltwater tank in the world (5.7 million gallons). SeaBase Alpha, a bi-level prototype undersea research facility, contains a visitors' center and information modules dedicated to six specific oceanographic subjects.

PREVIOUS PAGES AND LEFT: *The dramatic exterior of The Living Seas includes wavelike crests and troughs.* ABOVE: *Inside, visitors can watch a diver or join in other explorations of the sea.*

ENTERING WORLD SHOWCASE

Across the lagoon from Future World is the distinctive World Showcase, which can be reached by 66-foot water taxis, called the FriendShip launches, or on double-decker buses that circle the 1.3-mile World Showcase promenade, or by a long, relaxed stroll.

World Showcase underwent a transformation from the previously described 1975 concept to its execution in 1982. Instead of 30 interior pavilions in a gigantic single building, World Showcase opened as a consecutive series of buildings, featuring nine host countries (two more were added later). Much of this rethinking was indebted to the ideas of Harper Goff, a Disney Imagineer who had been art director on *20,000 Leagues Under the Sea* and had been instrumental in early Disneyland designs, such as the Jungle Cruise. Each pavilion makes use of the lagoon as a waterfront, adapts iconic national architecture to furnish the atmosphere of the host nation, and is staffed by citizens of the host countries, on a Disney-hosted college-level educational program.

MEXICO

OPPOSITE, NEAR RIGHT: *Although it is difficult to believe from this photograph, this Aztec pyramid is actually inside the Mexico pavilion, where it is set in the perpetual evening of the interior courtyard.* FAR RIGHT: *The exterior of the Mexico pavilion also resembles an Aztec temple.*

An Aztec-inspired pyramid surrounded by tropical foliage announces the Mexico pavilion. By the lagoon, the festive Cantina serves fast food and *cerveza.* Inside the cool, dark pyramid, visitors can view a variety of exhibits before entering the main section of the building. A quiet plaza, ringed with shops, looks across a waterway toward a volcano, seemingly ready to erupt. Near the waterway, the San Angel Inn offers atmospheric dining. To one side is the entry to El Rio del Tiempo (The River of Time), a six-minute boat trip that includes representations of Mexico's ancient, colonial, and modern cultures. The perpetual evening and relaxed mood of the courtyard are terrific examples of Imagineering art.

NORWAY

OPPOSITE, NEAR RIGHT: *This concept painting was the visual inspiration from which the Imagineers created the Norway pavilion.* FAR RIGHT: *Inside, visitors board dragon-headed longboats, for a journey through a mythical forest, under a North Sea oil rig during a fierce storm, and into the Geiranger fjord.*

The Norway pavilion joined World Showcase on May 6, 1988. Sponsored by a consortium of Norwegian corporations, the cobbled village square of the pavilion showcases architectural styles of towns like Bergen, Setesdal, and Oslo, including the Stave Church (which houses a gallery) and a castle (which houses a restaurant) modeled after Akershus, a 14th-century fortress in Oslo Harbor. The Norway pavilion also contains beautifully crafted rock and stone work, some of the finest ever fabricated by the Disney Imagineers.

The Norway attraction, called Maelstrom, is a 10-minute boat ride (in dragon-headed longboats), which begins in a 10th-century Viking village and journeys through a mythical forest populated by trolls, who curse the longboats and cause them to plummet backwards downriver. This unusual ride system is unique to this attraction. After the voyage, which also includes a storm under a North Sea oil rig and a trip to the Geiranger fjord, "survivors" are invited to watch an engaging five-minute 70mm film about the spirit of Norway and its people.

*The silhouettes of a Japanese* torii *gate and the Eiffel Tower share the horizon in a view that would seem out of place anywhere except World Showcase.*

## MEXICO

## NORWAY

CHINA

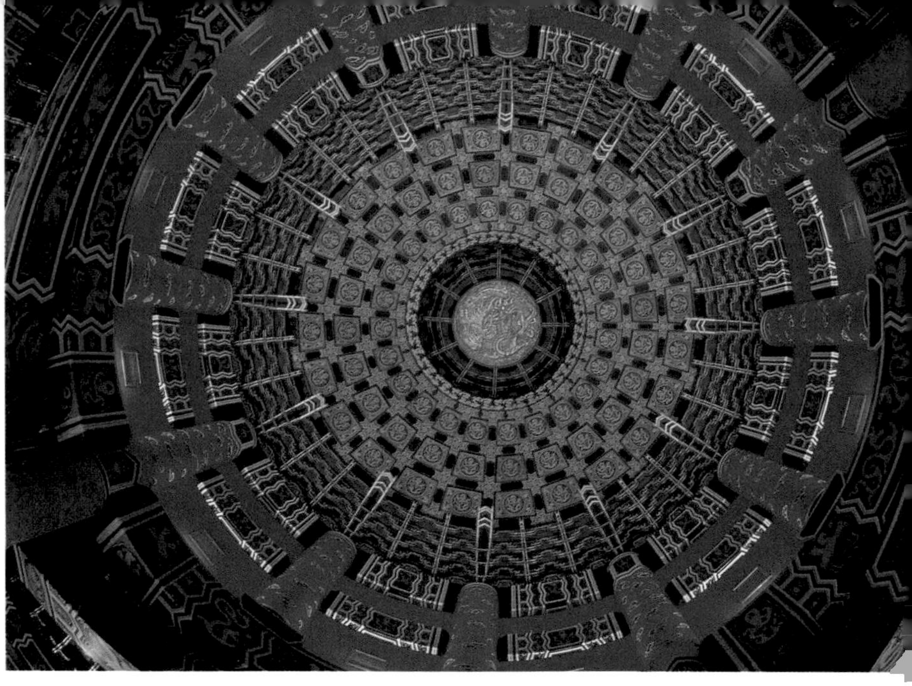

GERMANY

ITALY

## CHINA

Only in World Showcase is China so close to Norway. Beijing's Temple of Heaven is re-created in the China pavilion, and a calming serenity seems to permeate the space. The landscaping and gardens add to the overall sense of place, as does the "background score" of traditional Chinese music.

The main attraction at the China pavilion is a 19-minute Circle-Vision 360 film, *The Wonders of China: Land of Beauty, Land of Time.* The footage of such famous sights as the Forbidden City, the Great Wall of China, Mongolia, the Yangtze River, the Shilin Stone Forest, and the Great Buddha of Leshan is truly spectacular; the Disney crew was the first Western team ever to photograph some of the sites.

The building that houses the Circle-Vision theater is one of Imagineering's proudest re-creations. Based on the designs of the 1420 Hall of Prayer for Good Harvest in the Temple of Heaven, the building is laden with detail, extending from the stone floor to the gilded and painted ceiling. Indeed, there is so much detail that it truly takes hours to appreciate the meticulous workmanship.

OPPOSITE, FAR LEFT: *The China pavilion is a re-creation of Beijing's Temple of Heaven, including the circular Hall of Prayer for Good Harvest.* NEAR LEFT: *Inside, the painted and gilded ceiling is awe-inspiring in its rich detail.*

## GERMANY

South of the China pavilion the stair-stepped roofs, steeple, turrets, and castle walls of the Germany pavilion are visible. An amalgam of architectural design details from various cities all over Germany, the pavilion conveys an overall feeling of a fairy-tale alpine village of centuries past. The statue in the center of the *platz,* or town square, is St. George (patron saint of soldiers) slaying the dragon.

The boutiques and food service facilities (particularly the rowdy Biergarten Restaurant) are the main attractions at the Germany pavilion. A Rhine River attraction was originally planned, and a building was even built for it, but the attraction was never constructed. A pair of massive wooden doors at the rear of the Sommerfest outdoor cafe is the only indication of the show building behind the stone castle wall.

OPPOSITE, FAR LEFT: *In a square inside the Germany pavilion stands a statue of St. George slaying the dragon.* NEAR LEFT: *The Alpenhorns may be the quietest entertainment offered at the boisterous Biergarten Restaurant.*

## ITALY

A re-creation of the Venetian *campanile* of St. Mark's proclaims the presence of the Italy pavilion. A love letter to Venice, the Italy pavilion also features an exacting replica of the Doge's Palace, and its watefront along the World Showcase Lagoon is dressed with playful gondolas and their festive, barber-striped moorings.

In the central plaza of the pavilion, the Plaza del Teatro, live street theater in the style of the commedia dell'arte is performed. The pavilion's popular restaurant is L'Originale Alfredo di Roma, an impressive Florentine-styled dining room with the interior walls decorated with trompe l'oeil paintings copied from those of Veronese.

OPPOSITE, FAR LEFT: *Along the World Showcase Lagoon, the Italy pavilion pays homage to Venice with gondolas and barber-striped moorings.* CENTER: *The pavilion features such Venetian sites as the campanile of St. Mark's and the Doge's Palace.* NEAR LEFT: *A statue of Neptune is the centerpiece of a fountain inspired by Bernini's Trevi fountain in Rome.*

OPPOSITE, NEAR RIGHT: *Housed in an enormous Georgian-style brick building, the United States pavilion draws visitors to the back of the park.* FAR RIGHT: *Inside, Benjamin Franklin, along with Mark Twain, hosts The American Adventure. The two were chosen as iconic Americans—Franklin for his cheery gifts of insight and invention, Twain for his circumspect outlook and wry humor.*

## UNITED STATES

The uncharacteristically gigantic Georgian brick building that houses The American Adventure, presented by Coca-Cola and American Express, is a far cry from the original plan for the United States pavilion. The question of how to present the spirit of America daunted the Imagineers. The United States was not one of the original World Showcase pavilion concepts; it was to be a sleek two-level structure on stilts in a transitional area near Future World. As the host country, the United States was to have a walk-*under* facility, with an attraction above—a gateway to World Showcase. There was concern that placing the United States in the Showcase itself might appear arrogant, but that setting it apart might appear aloof. Finally, the Imagineers decided to celebrate the very spirit that could produce a project like EPCOT Center. The United States pavilion with its spectacular show, The American Adventure, would become the central focus of World Showcase.

To fit in with its World Showcase neighbors, the original contemporary-style U.S. facility (likened to the Hirshhorn Museum in Washington, D.C.) was abandoned in favor of a more traditionally "American" facade. On the pavilion waterfront, an outdoor amphitheater, the America Gardens Theater, was designed to host a variety of performances.

The show the Imagineers produced is striking and one of a kind. Hosted by Audio-Animatronics figures of Mark Twain and Benjamin Franklin, the spirit of the nation is portrayed from the landing of the *Mayflower* to the present, through an elaborate combination of film, special effects, music, Audio-Animatronics tableaux, and sets that rise, roll, and lower. The cast of characters includes Audio-Animatronics figures George Washington, Chief Joseph, Frederick Douglass, Franklin Roosevelt, Susan B. Anthony, John Muir, Will Rogers, and Alexander Graham Bell, as well as film appearances by Jackie Robinson, Marilyn Monroe, Margaret Mead, John F. Kennedy, Walt Disney, Ryan White, and Jim Henson. The 29-minute show pulls out all the stops, using just about every technique available to the Imagineers except a roller coaster.

## JAPAN

The *torii* gate is found throughout Japan at the entry to ancient shrines. A great vermilion *torii* on the shores of World Showcase Lagoon, adapted from the Itsukushima Shrine in Hiroshima Bay, is the entry to Disney's shrine to the architecture and heritage of Japan in World Showcase.

Looming 83 feet above the pavement is a pagoda, adapted from the seventh-century Horyuji Shrine at Nara. (Although similar to the Chinese pagodas that inspired them, Japanese pagodas use less color, less curve, and less ornamentation, emphasizing instead the grace of the designs and simplicity of line.) Its five stories symbolize earth, water, fire, wind, and sky; and the pagoda is topped by a *sorin* composed of nine rings, each with its own wind chimes.

## UNITED STATES

## JAPAN

ABOVE:

*Adapted from the Itsukushima Shrine in Hiroshima Bay, this* torii *is the entry to Japan in World Showcase.*

LEFT:

*This replica of the seventh-century Horyuji Shrine at Nara rises 83 feet. On top, each of the nine rings of the* sorin *has its own wind chimes.*

## MOROCCO

*The Morocco pavilion celebrates the country's architecture and ornament with inviting warm earth tones, green tile roofs, attractive geometric patterns, and rich textures.*

## FRANCE

*Approaching the France pavilion, visitors cross a replica of the Pont des Arts, a footbridge that once led from the Louvre to the quais of the Left Bank. The Eiffel Tower and mansard roofs leave little doubt that Paris is the inspiration for this pavilion.*

The pavilion contains a gallery, a restaurant, and a Mitsukoshi Department Store, housed in other replications of early Japanese architecture. Naturally, the meticulous Japanese art of landscape design is on full display throughout the pavilion grounds, although most of the plants are stand-ins for the actual Japanese varieties, since few Japanese plants could survive the Florida climate.

### MOROCCO

On the drawing boards along with the rest of the opening-day pavilions, the Morocco pavilion did not actually open until September 7, 1984, nearly two years after the rest of World Showcase. The pavilion is a true celebration of the architecture and ornamentation of Morocco, welcoming visitors with its warm earth tones and green tile roofs, as well as its inviting geometric patterns and sensual textures.

Following the pattern of many Moroccan cities, the pavilion is divided in two. The *ville nouvelle* (new city) contains a stunning replica of the Koutoubia minaret of Marrakesh, leading into a courtyard containing a replica of the Nejjarine Fountain, which in turn leads to the gated entrance of the Medina (old city). Nineteen *maalems* (Moroccan artisans) worked on the extensive mosaic art that can be seen throughout the pavilion. Altogether, nine tons of handmade enameled terra-cotta tile were used. There are faithful reproductions of the Bab Boujouloud gate in Fez, the minaret at Chella, and the bells of the Madrassa.

In addition to the atmospheric and evocative architecture, the pavilion contains a marketplace of crafted brasswork, hand-knotted Berber carpets, leather goods, furniture, and various crafts, as well as a tourist office, a gallery of art and artifacts, and a Moroccan restaurant.

*The extensive mosaic art on display in the Morocco pavilion is the work of 19* maalems *(Moroccan artisans), who came to Florida specifically for the project.*

### FRANCE

Paris is clearly the key influence for the France pavilion. The mansard roofs, casement windows, and chimney stacks are *très parisien*, recalling the designs of city planner Baron Georges-Eugène Haussmann. The looming ironwork of the Eiffel Tower evokes the City of Light. A sidewalk cafe, the rich smell of a boulangerie, a fine bistro, a park inspired by Georges Seurat's painting *A Sunday Afternoon on the Island of La Grande Jatte*, even an arcade designed after Hector Guimard's Art Nouveau entry arch for the Métro, add to the evocation of romance, charm, and elegance.

In the Fontainebleau-inspired Palais du Cinéma, an 18-minute panoramic travelogue, *Impressions de France*, is projected onto five contiguous projection surfaces 27½ feet wide by 21 feet high. Set to the music of Saint-Saëns, Debussy, Offenbach, and Satie, the film carries the audience on an enthralling photographic journey from Normandy, through the French Alps, to the Riviera.

Within the France pavilion, there is a wonderful replica of Les Halles, a once-beloved Parisian market, with overhead iron girders and skylights. And as visitors stroll north toward the United Kingdom pavilion, they cross a loving replica of the Pont des Arts, a footbridge that once led from the Louvre to the quais of the Left Bank. The Parisian originals have been torn down—Les Halles and the Pont des Arts exist only in memory and at World Showcase.

The adjacent International Gateway was created along with the EPCOT Resorts in 1990. This canal connects waterways of the hotels to World Showcase Lagoon, and a pedestrian walkway leads from the hotels to World Showcase Promenade.

### UNITED KINGDOM

On the waterfront of the United Kingdom pavilion is a proper British pub. On the lagoon side, the pub is reminiscent of a waterside saloon on the Thames River. On the street side, it's a neighborhood tavern in Soho. Called the Rose and Crown, it bears the dignified Latin motto, "Otium Cum Dignitate" ("Leisure with Dignity").

The pavilion is a cornucopia of re-created British architecture. High Street features Elizabethan, Tudor, and Victorian buildings. A replica of Henry VIII's Hampton Court Palace, complete with cartouche, houses a toy store. Elegant Belgrave Square row houses, formal gardens, a hedge maze, Hyde Park, Yorkshire and Regency buildings, even a Shakespearean cottage—all are part of the architectural tour. The melange of styles is made all the more fascinating by the ease with which the Imagineers have blended the diverse styles into a romantic fantasy of the United Kingdom.

### CANADA

Canada is the last pavilion in the World Showcase, combining the several traditions and geographic regions of the country into a setting that is at once startling in its diversity and inviting in its verticality. Towering above is the distinctive French gothic architecture of the Hôtel du Canada (modeled on Ottawa's Château Laurier). Alongside and beneath the chateau is EPCOT Center's Canadian Rocky Mountain, which houses a Circle-Vision theater. The Northwest Coast atmosphere is heightened by enormous totem poles and a native log house. There is also a miniature replica of the famed Butchart Gardens, a 30-foot waterfall, a restaurant, and the woodsman's haven of Salmon Island.

Through a miner's tunnel and into the mountain, *O Canada!*, the Circle-Vision 360 presentation, awaits. Another amazing example of this in-the-round presentation technique, *O Canada!* is a thrilling coast-to-coast voyage across the varied geography, wildlife, and spectacle of the Western Hemisphere's largest nation.

*Part of the extensive master planning of World Showcase is the seamless blending of disparate architectural styles, as in this stretch of waterfront for the United Kingdom and Canada.*

## UNITED KINGDOM

*In the United Kingdom pavilion, English street entertainment is provided by a group of "Pearlies," so named because of the hundreds of decorative pearl buttons adorning their colorful costumes.*

## CANADA

*In the Canada pavilion the towering Hôtel du Canada (modeled on Ottawa's Château Laurier), representing the French influence, contrasts with the Northwest Coast atmosphere created by gigantic totem poles and a native log house.*

*During the IllumiNations night-time spectacular, fireworks explode over the pin-lighted outlines of the pavilions around World Showcase Lagoon.*

ILLUMINATIONS

One regular feature of EPCOT Center that has come to be regarded as an attraction in itself is the nighttime spectacular, IllumiNations. Synchronized lights, laser beams, fountains, and fireworks all enliven World Showcase Lagoon, with pin-lighted pavilion outlines and a massive laser projection on the geosphere of Spaceship Earth at the show's finale.

EPCOT RENEWED

In 1994 Disney renewed its commitment to EPCOT Center's role as a discovery park, a permanent exposition of world culture and optimistic future living. Given the acceptance of "EPCOT" as a word, not just an acronym, the park was rechristened "Epcot," and the decision was made to reexamine its programming and content each year, and to promote the park in that way. Epcot '94, Epcot '95, and Epcot '96 have followed.

In the end, Epcot carries through much of Walt Disney's visionary philosophy, although in a decidedly different way than he intended. As one of Walt's closest lieutenants, John Hench, summarized in a 1993 interview:

> *Walt had this ambition to open this place which, when you really analyze it, was a place where people could get better information. He thought that all the evils of the world were because people didn't get the right informa-tion, so people didn't react right. People were capable of all kinds of evils because they were operating on the wrong information. So he thought he could build a place where he could straighten out some of those things, and when I think of the guts it took—it's so surprising to think of charging [admission] at the front gate, for a guy to come in to lose some of his prejudices.*

# CHAPTER FIVE

# DISNEY-MGM

# STUDIOS

CHOCOLATE
CROSSROADS

*The motion picture has become a necessity of life, a part of our balanced existence. It is not a negligible luxury.*

—WALT DISNEY

After EPCOT Center opened in 1982, growth at Walt Disney World slowed. The staggering cost and strain on the resources of Walt Disney World, Walt Disney Imagineering, and Walt Disney Productions left corporate management gun-shy. Though EPCOT Center was deemed a success, the officers of Walt Disney Productions were reluctant to commit the kind of resources it took to build EPCOT Center to further expand the Florida property. During the next few years, the Horizons and Morocco pavilions at EPCOT Center would open, development on The Living Seas would begin in earnest, but little else would even hit the drawing boards. Tokyo Disneyland, a joint venture with Oriental Land Company, had Disney employees hard at work on a landfill site in Tokyo Bay. In fact, Walt Disney Productions had bigger worries on the horizon.

*Roy E. Disney, vice chairman of The Walt Disney Company, in the mid-1980s.*

OPPOSITE:
*A nighttime view down Hollywood Boulevard, from the entry plaza of Disney-MGM Studios to the replica of Grauman's Chinese Theater.*

## TAKING STOCK

In March 1984 Roy E. Disney resigned after years of dissatisfaction with the manner in which Walt Disney Productions was being run. He had seen the company's profits slide from a high of $135 million in 1980 to $93 million in just three years. At first Roy planned to mastermind a takeover bid of the Disney company and sought the advice of longtime colleague Stanley Gold. To initiate the takeover, Gold called Frank Wells, a prominent entertainment attorney and former president of Warner Bros. The three men (a group known informally as the brain trust) met with Michael Milken, who would subsequently gain infamy as the Drexel Lambert "junk bond king." Milken assured the three that he could raise the $2 billion needed to take over Disney—but paying off the debt of the takeover would almost certainly mean selling off substantial portions of the company's assets. It was something that Roy Disney just couldn't do, and the brain trust backed away. Roy instead increased his stock holdings in Disney by 700,000 shares (more than 5 percent of the company).

New York financier Saul Steinberg, who had attempted several takeovers, including those of Quaker State Oil and Chemical Bank, took up the takeover bid. One of Steinberg's fiscal tactics was "greenmail," whereby he acquired large blocks of stock in attempted takeovers and sold the stock back to the company at a higher price, agreeing *not* to complete the takeover bid. Steinberg bought 6.3 percent of Disney's stock and in May 1984 launched a $1.2 billion bid to buy 49 percent of the company.

Ultimately, Disney found a friendly suitor, an investor who could buy a large enough block of stock to put the takeover out of Steinberg's fiscal reach, but who would remain true to the vision of the Disney board of directors. In May the board approved a stock trade that gave Sid Bass, a Texas billionaire, 8.9 percent (3.3 million shares) of Walt Disney Productions

*Disney's Caribbean Beach Resort.*

in exchange for his Florida real estate development company, Arvida. To displace Saul Steinberg, the Disney board paid $325.5 million for his Disney stock in June 1984. Just as Steinberg dropped out, Minneapolis investor Irwin Jacobs bought 6 percent of Walt Disney Productions and was reportedly preparing for a takeover.

Roy Disney and Stanley Gold threatened to sue Disney's board over the Arvida deal, since it substantially diluted Roy's stock holdings. The board countered by installing Disney, Gold, and Disney's brother-in-law, Peter Dailey, as members of the Disney board. The board then sent a decisive message to Wall Street with a radical management shift. Studio head (and Walt Disney's son-in-law) Ron Miller was asked to resign. On September 22, 1984, Frank Wells and former Paramount Pictures production head Michael Eisner were installed to head Walt Disney Productions. The two would share duties, Wells as president and chief operating officer, Eisner as chairman and chief executive officer.

### A NEW GENERATION OF LEADERSHIP

Among their many other operations, Eisner and Wells saw the Florida property as highly underdeveloped, particularly in the number of Disney-owned hotel rooms. They began a program of measured, but assertive, growth for Walt Disney World.

Between September 1984 and 1989, ambitious additions to Walt Disney World included *Captain EO*, Mickey's Birthdayland (now Mickey's Toontown Fair) at the Magic Kingdom, the Norway pavilion at EPCOT Center, Disney's Caribbean Beach Resort, Disney's Grand Floridian Beach Resort, Typhoon Lagoon water park, and the nightlife district Pleasure Island.

Early in 1985 Eisner and Wells authorized a third theme park for the property. The creation of a third, separate gated attraction would encourage more visits by Florida residents and longer stays by out-of-towners. This park would be planned on a smaller scale than EPCOT Center, with controlled growth in reaction to anticipated demand.

*Disney's Yacht Club Resort, designed by well-known architect Robert A. M. Stern.*

### THE THIRD GATE

The idea for the third gate actually began during the designing of EPCOT Center. The Imagineers had been planning a new pavilion for Future World, focusing on the movies and Hollywood. Not long after they started at Disney, Eisner and Wells saw plans for this "Movie Pavilion." As presented by Walt Disney Imagineering, the pavilion show was a ride-through of great moments from classic movies like *The Wizard of Oz* and *Casablanca*. Legendary Disney animator Ward Kimball worked extensively on an ancillary attraction called Mickey's Movieland, which would portray, in Audio-Animatronics tableaux, a comic behind-the-scenes history of the making of early Mickey Mouse cartoons.

Eisner saw no reason to limit this basic concept to a single pavilion in an already-existing park. The idea lent itself to expansions and elabora-

## CARIBBEAN BEACH RESORT

This time, there's nary a pirate in sight, but Disney returned to the Caribbean on October 1, 1988, with the opening of Disney's Caribbean Beach Resort.

The first of a new category of moderate-priced hotels on Walt Disney World property (and with 2,112 rooms on 200 acres, one of the largest hotels in Florida), the Caribbean Beach was created to meet a tourist demand for Disney-style themed accommodations on Disney property, without luxury amenities and prices.

Located southeast of Epcot, six tropically themed, brightly colored resort villages surround a 42-acre man-made lake. The villages are composed of clusters of two-story buildings themed in Caribbean styles—Barbados, Martinique, Aruba, Jamaica, Trinidad North, and Trinidad South—blending cool pastel walls, white wood railings, and vividly colored corrugated metal roofs. A mile-and-a-half-long promenade circles the lake and is used by pedestrians, joggers, and bicyclists.

The entrance to the Caribbean Beach Resort is off Buena Vista Drive, and guest check-in and resort services are centrally located in a welcome center, built in the style of a Caribbean customs house. Old Port Royale, the architectural focal point of the resort, has the feel of a Spanish fortress, with stone walls and pirate cannons amid lush tropical vegetation. The resort's shops, game room, lounge, and food court (six counter-service restaurants) are all located here.

Footbridges over the lake connect the mainland with the one-acre Parrot Cay Island, which contains several children's play areas and scenic walkways. The resort also offers small sailboats, canoes, and other watercraft, as well as bicycles, for rental.

The success of this resort, which combines Disney-quality "show" with moderate rates, spurred the development of another, similar resort on the property—Dixie Landings and Port Orleans—in 1992.

## YACHT AND BEACH CLUB RESORTS

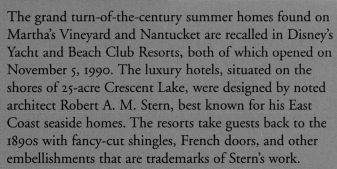

The grand turn-of-the-century summer homes found on Martha's Vineyard and Nantucket are recalled in Disney's Yacht and Beach Club Resorts, both of which opened on November 5, 1990. The luxury hotels, situated on the shores of 25-acre Crescent Lake, were designed by noted architect Robert A. M. Stern, best known for his East Coast seaside homes. The resorts take guests back to the 1890s with fancy-cut shingles, French doors, and other embellishments that are trademarks of Stern's work.

Although adjacent and complementary, the hotels have distinctive architectural styles. Each has its own entrance motif, main lobby, restaurants, and retail shops.

In the Yacht Club, the nautical feel of oak floors, antique chandeliers, and rich millwork and brass evoke New England summer days. The 635 spacious rooms and 30 suites are decorated in blues and whites. All have French doors that open onto porches or balconies.

The pale blue and white Beach Club is "stick-style," the prevalent architecture for seaside wooden cottages in the 1860s and 1870s. White wicker furniture, 24-foot ceilings, natural French limestone floors, and a seashell motif carry through the theme.

The 584 rooms and 29 suites have a summer cottage ambiance with cool colors, scattered seashells, and French doors to outdoor porches and a white sand beach.

Landscaping helps set the New England stage, with a variety of deciduous trees, including magnolias, Japanese elms, Bradford pear trees, and crape myrtle. Gardenias and roses bloom in intimate brick courtyards. An expansive croquet lawn at the Yacht Club Resort goes with the relaxed, leisurely spirit of the 1870s, and the resort's marina lighthouse welcomes guests home after a day at Walt Disney World.

The seacoast imagery continues in Stormalong Bay, a two-and-a-half-acre water recreation area reminiscent of a Nantucket beach. It features a life-size shipwreck with water slides, snorkeling in a sandy lagoon, and a meandering swimming area, which seems to flow into the surrounding lake.

Adjacent to the Yacht Club Resort there is also a 52,000-square-foot convention center, which includes a 36,000-square-foot ballroom capable of seating up to 2,800 for dinner. Together the two resorts have four restaurants, four lounges, a grill, a soda shop, two boutiques, a health club, a beauty salon, boat rentals, tennis, volleyball, croquet, and a game arcade.

Resort guests can walk or take a tram directly to the International Gateway at World Showcase in Epcot, and boat transportation goes directly from the hotels to Disney-MGM Studios.

*Michael Eisner (front), as chairman and chief executive officer, and Frank Wells, as president and chief operating officer, take charge of Walt Disney Productions in September 1984.*

tions on so many levels that the concept was exploded into a movie studio design. Within a few months, Imagineers had developed a park design including sound stages with grandstands for live audiences, a stunt show, and a tour of the movie lot.

Movie studio tours were certainly nothing new. The idea traces its way back to 1915, when Universal Pictures president Carl Laemmle, in an effort to increase revenue for his new 235-acre Universal City, actively promoted his studio as a tourist attraction. For 25 cents, visitors could see the latest Universal films being made. After a tour of the studio's back-lot streets, visitors could have lunch at an on-lot restaurant called Dine with the Stars. By 1964 Universal had turned the studio tour into an elaborate tram tour of the extensive Universal back-lot sets and a Western stunt show. (The phrase "When in Hollywood, Visit Universal Studios Tour" was frequently seen at the end of Universal Pictures releases and in Universal newspaper advertisements.) Most Hollywood studios offered (and continue to offer) lot tours, but except for the Universal ones, they were strictly small-group, VIP affairs. In the 1970s Universal Studios began to regard their studio tour as a real tourist attraction. By the 1980s, following the marketing lead of Disneyland, Universal had become a theme park.

Even Disney's interaction with the studio tour concept could be traced back nearly four decades. A Walt Disney studio tour and a specially constructed radio and television broadcast facility were planned as part of the Mickey Mouse Park layout that Walt Disney had begun developing in the late 1940s and early 1950s.

### CREATING THE STUDIO

Sparked by the enthusiasm of their new leadership, the Imagineers began their design process. The whole aura of the movies—the mythology of 20th-century humankind—was the Imagineers' cultural well. The glamorous Hollywood of the collective consciousness and the rich early-20th-century architectural history of Los Angeles were publicly revered (and in the public domain), completely at their creative disposal.

Eisner and Wells gave them even more to work with. On June 27, 1985, Walt Disney Productions and MGM/UA Entertainment signed an agreement giving Disney the exclusive rights to use up to 250 MGM/UA films at any one time. Thirty-five films, including *Singin' in the Rain, The Wizard of Oz*, the James Bond series, and *Gone With the Wind*, were treated separately and required special licensing for use. The pièce de résistance in this deal, however, was the Disney acquisition of a license for the world-famous Metro-Goldwyn-Mayer name and Leo the Lion logo, for unlimited use on stationery, posters, and advertisements. (The low cost to Disney of the overall MGM/UA deal reportedly infuriated MGM owner Kirk Kerkorian, who had not been a part of the negotiations. In 1988 Kerkorian filed a lawsuit in an attempt to nullify the deal, but this maneuver failed.)

# GRAND FLORIDIAN BEACH RESORT

Disney's Grand Floridian Beach Resort, which opened along the shores of Seven Seas Lagoon on June 28, 1988, recalls the splendor of grand Victorian hotels. The eastern seaboard of Florida had been turned into a winter resort mecca by Standard Oil tycoon Henry M. Flagler in the 1890s, when he extended his rail lines south into the panhandle and founded Palm Beach. Circus owner John Ringling created a similar winter haven in Sarasota, on Florida's west coast.

The Grand Floridian design draws from the most easily recognized stylistic patterns of Victorian architecture: towers, dormers, cupolas, exposed gable trusses, and band-sawed gingerbread. The Grand Floridian is life at a leisurely pace—a stroll along broad verandahs, wicker rockers beneath lazy ceiling fans, palm trees, and white sand beaches.

The design team visited the Bellevue Biltmore in Clearwater, Florida; the Grand Hotel on Mackinac Island, Michigan; and the Del Coronado in San Diego, California. The Bellevue Biltmore provided ideas for materials, dormer shapes, and size. The Del Coronado (the location used for the film *Some Like It Hot*) has similar colors and some similar elements—the Del and the Grand Floridian are sisters of the same Victorian family. The Grand Hotel (the hotel used in the film *Somewhere in Time*) fascinated the designers because its size didn't affect its ambiance and character—it is truly grand without overpowering the guests.

Another design challenge (one that none of the other hotels faced) was a sleek, modern monorail stopping at the doorstep. The designers decided that a Victorian train station design was in keeping with the reference to Flagler, who extended Florida's rail lines. Guests arrive at the train station, enter the grand resort destination with its lofty reception lobby, and relax in the recreational courtyard with its broad lawn and gardens—all common experiences in the destination resorts of old.

The five-story lobby features stained-glass domes, chandeliers, an aviary, potted palms, and a grand piano; often a parlor orchestra plays from a musician's gallery. A grand staircase and a cage elevator offer access to the second-story shops and restaurants.

The Grand Floridian features five restaurants, two lounges, a snack bar, four shops, an arcade, a child-care facility, a swimming pool, a children's activity area, a health club, and a marina. In 1992 an adjacent 27,037-square-foot convention center was opened.

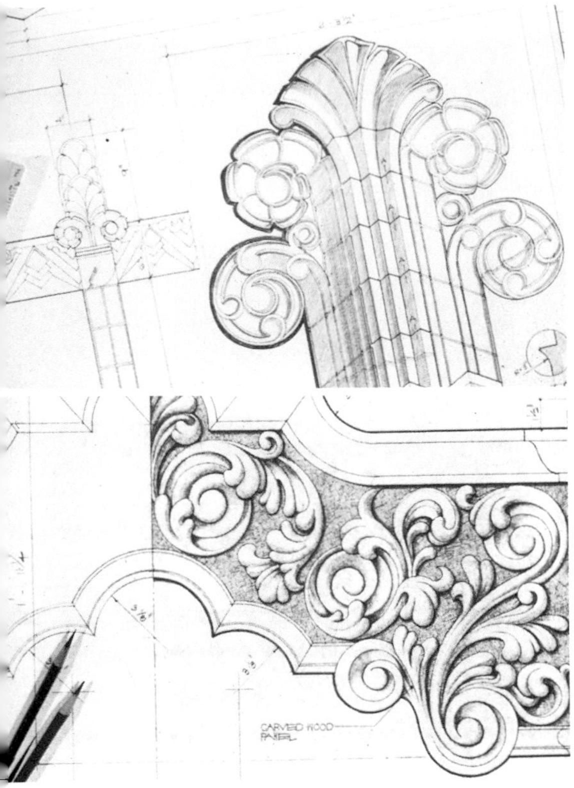

*Design details help create the magic of "a Hollywood that never was—and always will be."*

On July 8, 1985, Michael Eisner and Florida governor Bob Graham appeared together at a press conference in Tallahassee to announce the plans for the Disney-MGM Studios project. There would be a ride-through Audio-Animatronics attraction called Great Moments at the Movies. There would be entertaining demonstration exhibits in the Video Theater. There would be two live stunt shows: one showcasing comedy stunts; the other, the Epic Stunt Show, demonstrating giant mechanical stunts. There would be an area called Disney Archives, showcasing the history of Walt Disney Productions in an interactive exhibit, and a demonstration of Disney Animation. Michael Eisner strongly felt that a movie studio without actual production would leave visitors feeling cheated, so a small production facility was planned, including a television stage (for the taping of programs for The Disney Channel, perhaps). The initial Disney-MGM Studios plan was justifiably conservative. Expansion could come easily if an interested audience existed. There was certainly no shortage of ideas inspired by Hollywood and the movies.

In fact, a relatively young team of Imagineers was going nuts in Glendale, re-creating favorite landmarks from their L.A. backyard and actualizing visions of a Hollywood that didn't exist—had never existed—except as a notion. They reviewed miles of film and conducted dozens of architectural field trips to choose the right imagery to communicate this romantic Hollywood immediately to visitors.

Interestingly, one inspiration for the new park was Disneyland. Imagineers cited the importance of the human scale, warmth, and feeling of intimacy inherent in the original Magic Kingdom. The hub-and-spoke design of Disneyland would be replicated. But Main Street here would be the *movies'* main street, Hollywood Boulevard. Like Disneyland, at the hub a palace would beckon visitors—a movie palace, the world-famous Grauman's Chinese Theater.

The site for Disney-MGM was selected on the south side of Buena Vista Drive, south of EPCOT Center and east of World Drive. The development of Disney-MGM Studios here (along with the new Caribbean Beach Resort and Typhoon Lagoon) would fill out a connection between the Disney Village and the EPCOT Resorts. The 135-acre site was prepared and construction began in 1986.

The Walt Disney Story in the Magic Kingdom once again became a preview center, this time for the Disney-MGM Studios Theme Park. The preview film featured a typical family visit to the new movie studio park; display areas presented detailed models; and concept art and a demonstration of Disney animation was given.

The initial conservatism in the design of Disney-MGM Studios began to crack by 1986. The Imagineering team continued to come up with winning ideas for attractions, and the scale of the project began to grow, continuing to expand until the project opening and beyond. The studio production facility was increased to three sound stages, a postproduction audio and video facility, a wardrobe department, and a property department. These buildings were planned with glass-partitioned accessways to let visitors watch daily studio activities in progress. The back lot was expanded to include a thrilling special-effects show, Catastrophe Canyon, complete with a flash flood, earthquake, and exploding oil tankers. The proposed display on Disney Animation became a full-scale animation production unit of Walt Disney Feature Animation. By the time the new theme park opened in May 1989 (the changes in scale had delayed the scheduled October 1988 opening), total costs had accumulated to more than $500 million.

Actual production began at Disney-MGM Studios even before its official opening, when a Disney TV sequel/series pilot, *Splash, Too*, set up shop in the new studio's back lot on February 22, 1988. Since then, dozens of movies and television shows have been filmed and taped at Disney-MGM Studios, including "Ed McMahon's Star Search," "Wheel of Fortune," *Honey, I Blew Up the Kid*, *Quick Change*, *Passenger 57*, and "The Mickey Mouse Club." (The first film shot at Walt Disney World was the 1976 Disney adventure *Treasure of Matecumbe*, which had shot Everglades scenes in near-by Kissimmee and filmed its final scenes on a Bay Lake beach.)

*Unsuspecting visitors on the Backstage Tram Tour stop in a set replicating a barren desert canyon—Catastrophe Canyon—where they are caught in such special-effects dramas as a flash flood.*

*Opening Celebrations.* TOP: *From left, Michael Eisner, Chewbacca, Carrie Fisher, an Ewok, George Lucas, another Ewok, Mark Hamill, and C3PO at the opening of Star Tours on December 15, 1989.* BOTTOM: *Bette Midler and Kevin Costner take part in the handprint ceremony in the forecourt of Grauman's Chinese Theater.*

OPENING THE DOORS

The opening press event for the Disney-MGM Studios on May 1, 1989, was the largest in Walt Disney World history. *Newsweek* had published an extensive cover story touting the project a few weeks earlier. Full-page advertisements appeared in *People*, and four-page ads were published in *Time* and *Newsweek*. Although it rained throughout opening day, the new park was packed, and auto traffic backed up for miles outside the parking lot. The lot was closed only half an hour after opening. Hundreds of radio and television broadcasts took place around the attractions. "Streetmosphere" characters and bands kept the large crowds on long lines entertained. Celebrities were on hand for the dedication of each attraction. George Lucas, Bette Midler, and Robin Williams put in appearances. A two-hour NBC special had aired the night before, starring Harry Anderson, George Burns, Ann Miller, and Mickey Rooney, and featuring cameos by Jane Fonda, James Stewart, Ronald Reagan, Margaret Thatcher, and Lech Walesa. Entertainment legend Bob Hope cut the ceremonial ribbon, and Michael Eisner proudly read the dedication plaque:

> *The world you have entered was created by The Walt Disney Company and is dedicated to Hollywood—not a place on a map, but a state of mind that exists wherever people dream and wonder and imagine, a place where illusion and reality are fused by technological magic. We welcome you to a Hollywood that never was—and always will be.*

The Disney-MGM Studios Theme Park was an instant success. Throughout the summer of 1989, the overflowing parking lot closed early. Park closing hours were extended from 6:00 P.M. to midnight every night. Imagineers scrambled to add more floor space. Back-lot sets that were meant to be viewed only from trams were opened to foot traffic to improve crowd flow. Future park expansion plans were immediately put into action. In the meantime, the park was able to handle overflowing crowds by quickly adding several live shows. Trailers were brought in to accommodate the already-expanding animation department.

BACK TO OLD HOLLYWOOD

"The show starts on the sidewalk" is a phrase coined in the heyday of the movie palace, by theater magnate Marcus Loew. The show at Disney-MGM Studios certainly starts on the sidewalk with the buildings themselves.

Visitors to Disney-MGM are immediately immersed in an old Hollywood feel. The magnificent streamlined main gate with its flagpole pylons is a reproduction of the facade of the 1935 Pan-Pacific Auditorium in Los Angeles. The original spectacular landmark was lost in 1989 to vandalism, fire, and civic neglect, but it lives on here.

Within the gate, visitors are standing at the foot of Hollywood Boulevard, with Grauman's Chinese Theater ahead. The Hollywood Boulevard at Disney-MGM Studios is *certainly* a fantasy one, a Hollywood too organized, too attractive, too *clean* to have ever been real. It is the Hollywood of vacation postcards and old radio shows and orange groves and fan magazines. But it is based on real Los Angeles structures and real cultural elements of the Hollywood life.

In the entry plaza is a souvenir and information shop, topped by a distinctive tower and globe, a reproduction of the entry plaza to the Crossroads of the World. A Hollywood landmark at 6671 Sunset Boulevard, the Crossroads was one of the first shopping plazas, combining a nautical motif with a European Village shopping area. The original still stands—but only at Disney-MGM is the spire's globe topped by Mickey Mouse.

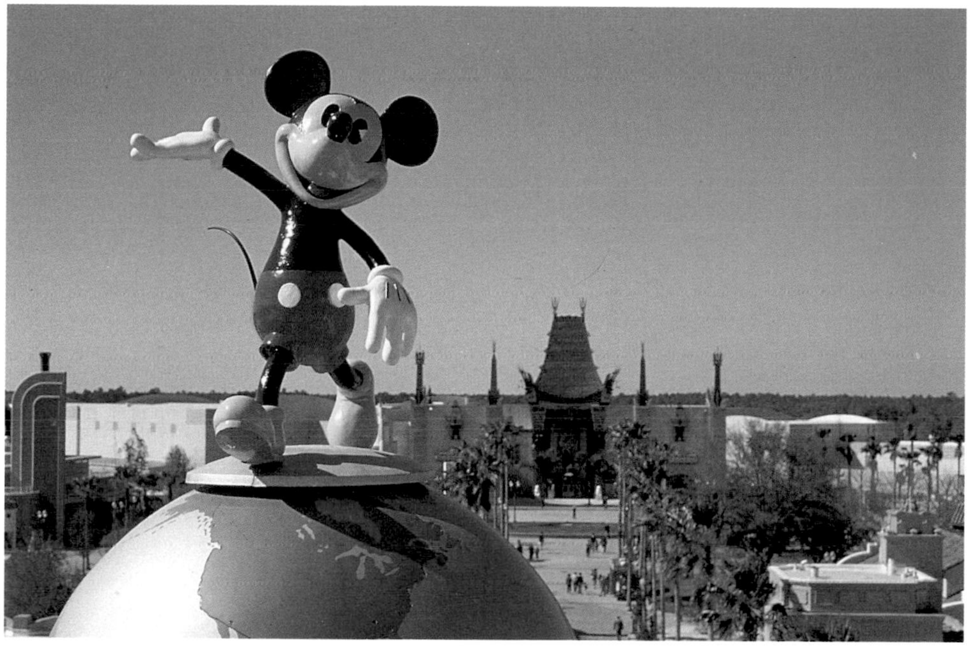

ABOVE:
*The entry plaza to Disney-MGM Studios features a replica of the globe tower at Crossroads of the World, a Hollywood landmark. Unlike the original, however, this version has Mickey Mouse on top of the world.*

LEFT:
*Hollywood Boulevard evokes the feel of Hollywood that is shared in cultural memory. It may never have been this way, but we imagine it was.*

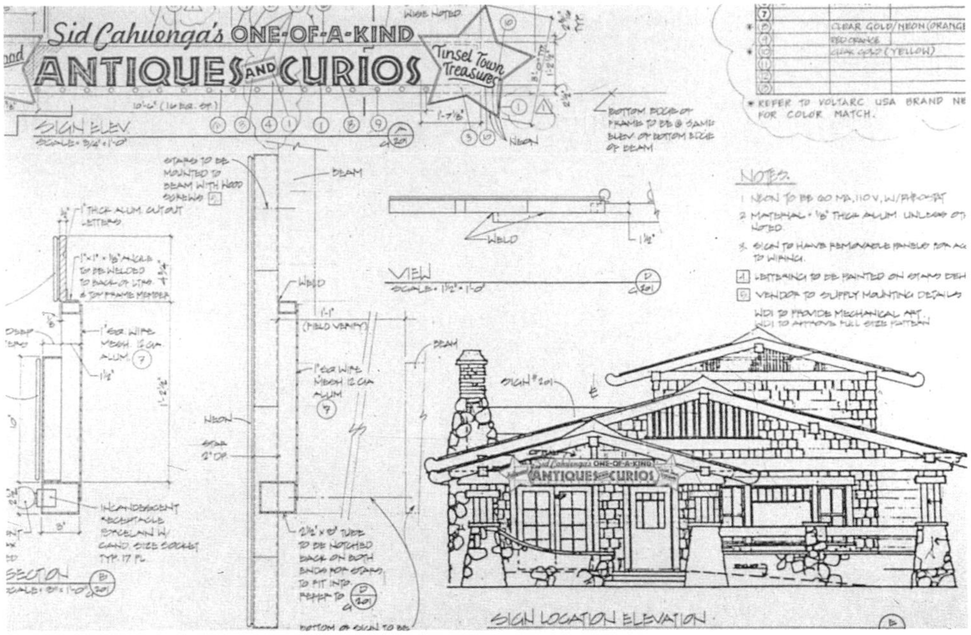


*Plans for Sid Cahuenga's One-of-a-Kind.*

Sid Cahuenga's One-of-a-Kind is to the west of the entry plaza. In a cluttered Craftsman-style bungalow, poor Sid ekes out an existence by selling antiques, curios, movie memorabilia, and collectibles out of his living room. ("Cahuenga" is the name of both a mountain pass and street running through the heart of Hollywood.) This kind of bungalow shop was actually once a common sight in Hollywood. As commercial development swallowed up residential streets, dozens of "Sid Cahuengas" could be found. Even today, many former residences house luggage shops (1359 North La Brea Avenue), florists, even production companies. (The idea, although not the architectural style, for this home/store came from the Janes House, the last residence on the commercial strip of Hollywood Boulevard. Although it has been incorporated into a mini-mall, the Janes House still stands, at 6541 Hollywood Boulevard.)

Directly across from Sid Cahuenga's is Oscar's Super Service, a tip of the cap to the car culture that was born (and still thrives) in Los Angeles. A 1947 Buick has pulled up to the service island, and a vintage billboard tops the service bay. The helpful service station of days gone by is the perfect setting for park services like stroller and wheelchair rental, lockers, infant needs, telephones, and postage stamp sales.

The Darkroom is an Art Deco icon of programmatic architecture (often called "California Crazy," programmatic buildings represent figures and objects, whether portraying what is sold inside or just for fun). The original of this camera shop housed behind a giant camera was built in Los Angeles at 5730 Wilshire Boulevard in 1938.

The intricate Art Deco glazed-tile facade of the Celebrity 5 & 10 draws its design (although not its color styling) from the classic J. J. Newberry store at 6600 Hollywood Boulevard (now the home of the

*A nighttime view of Mickey's of Hollywood and other buildings along Hollywood Boulevard.*

Hollywood Toy Company). The color styling of the Hollywood Newberry store is similar to the turquoise colors used across the street, on the southwest facade of Keystone Clothier.

Nearby, Sweet Success replicates a portion of a truly spectacular two-block-long Spanish Colonial Revival structure that still stands in the 3400 block of Sixth Street (at Kenmore Avenue) in Los Angeles.

On the west side of the street, Mickey's of Hollywood replicates several Hollywood facades, including a Spanish Revival commercial block at 6601 Hollywood Boulevard, an elegant black marble and gilt facade at 5209 Wilshire Boulevard, and the once-stylish street frontage of the old Max Factor building, facing Highland Avenue at 1660 North Highland.

The facade of Pluto's Palace is modeled after the distinctively marqueed front of an animal hospital at 940 North Highland Avenue in Hollywood. To the north of Pluto's, the Art Deco rotunda on the north side of Disney & Co. is derived from a Deco building at 6424 Santa Monica Boulevard (at Cole Avenue), which now houses 525 Post Production.

The northwest side of Keystone Clothier re-creates a streamlined building at the southeast corner of Cahuenga Avenue in the 6300 block of Hollywood Boulevard, now known as the Julian Medical Building.

The Hollywood Brown Derby pays homage to the second Brown Derby restaurant (1929), once located at 1624 Vine Street, just south of Hollywood Boulevard. While this second restaurant didn't have the famous derby-shaped architecture of the original Wilshire Boulevard restaurant, it was even more of a star magnet than its predecessor, due to its location close to several of the major film and broadcasting studios. (It wasn't unheard of for actors to arrive for lunch in full costume and makeup.) The Derby, founded by Wilson Mizner and Herbert Somborn, was passed to Robert H.

*Gene Siskel (left) and Roger Ebert continue a Brown Derby tradition, sitting in a booth beneath celebrity caricatures (originally drawn by Eddie Vitch in exchange for meals).*

OPPOSITE:
*Sorcery in the Sky fireworks explode behind the famous facade of Grauman's Chinese Theater, which looks just like the Hollywood original.*

Cobb in 1934. (This is the Cobb of the Derby's signature Cobb salad.) The most famous regular customers sat on the desirable north side of the dining room, in booths beneath celebrity caricatures (drawn originally by Eddie Vitch, who traded them for meals). The Derby also began the very Hollywood practice of paging diners and delivering telephones to their tables. These details, as well as the solid, elegant ambiance—and terrific food—are beautifully re-created in the Disney-MGM Brown Derby. The furniture, fittings, and caricatures were copied from many of the originals still in the possession of Walter Scharfe and Elizabeth Khittle-Scharfe, who own the contents (and the trade name "Hollywood Brown Derby") from the Vine Street restaurant.

At the end of Florida's Hollywood Boulevard is Grauman's Chinese Theater, which looks for all the world like the genuine article located at 6925 Hollywood Boulevard (albeit much tidier). The Imagineers used the blueprints of the original 1927 Meyer and Holler building for reference, and the facade is built to full scale, rather than in the interpretive scale of the rest of the theme park's Hollywood Boulevard. (The 22-foot central roof section was constructed separately and hoisted into place by crane.)

The theater houses The Great Movie Ride (developed under the working name "Great Moments from the Movies"), presented by Coca-Cola. The queue area winds through a reproduction of the Chinese Theater lobby, with authentic film memorabilia on display, and into an auditorium, where preview trailers of the films depicted within the ride itself are unspooled on a giant screen. In the loading area, passengers board large-scale vehicles for a tour of classic film scenes, re-created in Audio-Animatronics tableaux. Films represented include Busby Berkeley's *Footlight Parade* (1933), *The Public Enemy* (1931), *Singin' in the Rain* (1952), *The Wizard of Oz* (1939), *Mary Poppins* (1964),

*Hand- and footprints are another Hollywood tradition translated to Florida. The original honorary "cement ceremony" was begun by Sid Grauman on April 15, 1927.*

MOVIE RIDE

WHISKY
WHISKY
WHISKY
WHISKY

*Alien* (1979), *Raiders of the Lost Ark* (1981), and *Casablanca* (1942). The finale of the ride is a film montage by acclaimed director Chuck Workman.

To the west of the epic central plaza is Lakeside Circle, with the man-made Echo Lake shimmering in its center. Echo Lake refers to an actual man-made lake near downtown L.A., Echo Park Lake, adjacent to the Edendale Studio of Mack Sennett's Keystone Pictures. Dozens of silent comedies were shot on this lily-strewn pond.

Alongside the lake there are two more examples of programmatic architecture. Min and Bill's Dockside Diner, a food service facility, is housed in a boat. Min and Bill are characters played by Marie Dressler and Wallace Beery, from a 1930 film of the same name. Dressler won the Academy Award for her performance.

The other lakeside building is Dinosaur Gertie's Ice Creams of Extinction. The building pays homage to California Crazy roadside architecture as well as pioneering animator Winsor McCay and his revolutionary 1914 animated cartoon, *Gertie the Dinosaur.*

The Hollywood & Vine Cafeteria is situated on the south side of Echo Lake. This spectacularly Spartan eatery recalls the cafeterias of the '30s, '40s, and '50s—once standard fare, before the dawn of fast food. Admittedly, the cafeteria culture of New York never fully caught on in Hollywood (Clifton's Cafeterias, which still operate today, were the L.A. equivalent of New York's Horn & Hardart or Chock Full O' Nuts). But the Hollywood &

*Echo Lake, with Min and Bill's Dockside Diner in back and Dinosaur Gertie's Ice Creams of Extinction in front.*

OPPOSITE:
*Among the many sights of The Great Movie Ride, a tour of classic film scenes re-created in Audio-Animatronics tableaux, are (clockwise from top left): Grauman's Chinese Theater, which houses the ride; Egyptian temple scene; the Wicked Witch of the West; and Gangster Alley.*

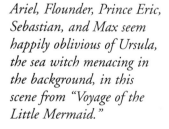

*The 50s Prime Time Cafe, with a TV at every table.*

Vine draws inspiration from a popular cafeteria that once stood at 1725 North Vine, near Hollywood Boulevard. The cafeteria (which was once the Hollywood Branch Post Office) closed in the 1980s, and the vacant structure burned down. Along with its appetizingly institutional interior design, the Disney-MGM Hollywood & Vine Cafeteria contains magnificent murals and photographs of old Hollywood.

West of the Hollywood & Vine, the architecture progresses to the modern Los Angeles of Richard Neutra, Pierre Koenig, and Frank Lloyd Wright. Here, appropriately enough, is the 50s Prime Time Cafe, a playful themed restaurant where every seating area is a tribute to mom, meatloaf, the color turquoise, and Formica™—with a TV at every table.

## THROUGH THE STUDIO GATE

Back across the central plaza is the studio gate, the formal entrance to the working studio. (Initially, the delineation between the working studio and the theme park was stronger, but expansion has necessarily blurred the line.) Much of the architecture and color styling was inspired by the original Kem Weber styles at the Walt Disney Studios in Burbank, California.

Within the studio gate is a courtyard, to the south of which is the Soundstage restaurant, a cafeteria-style affair ostensibly established on a sound stage floor amid movie sets and catered by a Hollywood craft services catering company. Initially, the sets were those of the Plaza Hotel from the 1988 Touchstone comedy *Big Business*. These sets were replaced by ones inspired by *Beauty and the Beast* in 1990, and then *Aladdin* in 1992, as well as later releases. A cocktail lounge, called the Catwalk Bar, is located in the lighting grids and rafters above the stage floor.

To the north is the Walt Disney Theater, originally used as a preview theater at the end of the studio walking tour. Here, guests could sit in air-conditioned comfort and see previews of the latest Disney film releases. In early 1990 the preview theater was relocated to a newly constructed auditorium, and the Walt Disney Theater became the venue for "Here Come the Muppets," a live stage show featuring costumed characters of the Jim

*Ariel, Flounder, Prince Eric, Sebastian, and Max seem happily oblivious of Ursula, the sea witch menacing in the background, in this scene from "Voyage of the Little Mermaid."*

*A set designer's drawing* (LEFT) *of the New York Street on the Disney-MGM Studios back lot and the finished back lot* (RIGHT) *in use by a film crew.*

Henson gang, which premiered May 25, 1990. "Here Come the Muppets" was replaced by the "Voyage of the Little Mermaid" show, which premiered on January 7, 1992. This 15-minute show combines live action, puppetry, lighting, sound, and special effects to retell the tale of Ariel and Prince Eric from the 1989 animated blockbuster.

Nearby, The Magic of Disney Animation is one of the most intelligent, evocative, and entertaining Disney attractions. The entry lobby features displays of Oscar statuettes and drawings, paintings, and other original animation art from classic Disney films, as well as an opportunity for a sneak peek of concept sketches and character models from upcoming features. The introduction to the attraction is a nine-minute film, titled *Back to Neverland.* Starring Walter Cronkite and Robin Williams, the film is a succinct explanation of the animation process. After the film, visitors walk through working animation studios. The finale of the tour is a short film montage of great moments from Disney animation.

A 25-minute Backstage Studio Tour begins with a presentation of the history of the Walt Disney Studios (hosted by Carol Burnett and Tom Selleck) shown on monitors in the queue area. Visitors board open-air trams, hosted by studio tour guides. The tram tour includes production bungalows, the wardrobe department, and the camera, props, lighting, and scene shops. A spin around the back-lot residential street features sets used in *Ernest Saves Christmas* and the homes from "The Golden Girls" and "Empty Nest." The tram stops in a set replicating a barren desert canyon, Catastrophe Canyon, a tour de force of special effects, including pyrotechnics and a flash flood. The tour concludes with a ride through a New York street set (if no filming is taking place, visitors can walk along the street).

The other half of the Backstage Studio Tour is the Inside the Magic Special Effects & Production Tour, a 40-minute walking tour featuring interactive demonstrations of several different types of special effects, including

*A graceful sculpture of Mickey Mouse climbing winding motion picture film stands at the entrance to The Magic of Disney Animation.*

*The Inside the Magic Special Effects & Production Tour engages visitors with different types of special effects. It originally included the flight of the bumble bee from* Honey, I Shrunk the Kids.

BELOW:
*Special effects come to life on the back lot, as this visitor-skipper of the* Miss Fortune *finds out.*

OPPOSITE, CLOCKWISE FROM TOP LEFT: *The 130-foot Disney-MGM Studios water tower with its 5,000-pound mouse ears; the streamlined tower of Superstar Television; the Monster Sound Show, where visitors participate in a demonstration of film sound-effects techniques; the Indiana Jones Epic Stunt Spectacular, which lives up to its name.*

water effects and pyrotechnics. Visitors are allowed on enclosed viewing catwalks, from which filming on studio sound stages can be seen. New for 1996 is an area that houses the sets from the live-action film *101 Dalmations.* Guests have the chance to stroll around the sets and learn about the production of the film.

Disney-MGM Studios production facilities include three sound stages; production offices; complete wardrobe, property, camera, lighting, and scenic capabilities; back-lot sets; and postproduction and editing facilities.

All the old Hollywood movie studios had water towers on their lots, for heating, cooling, and emergency uses. Most studios also used these towers as skyline billboards for their studio logos. Disney-MGM Studios wouldn't be complete without a water tower, and the water tower wouldn't be Disney

if it were just a water tower. The 130-foot Disney-MGM Studios tower sports a pair of 5,000-pound mouse ears, hence its playful moniker "The Earffel Tower." The water tower is strictly a landmark.

Back in the central plaza, the streamlined tower of Superstar Television, presented by SONY, is clearly visible. Visitors to Superstar Television get a cursory demonstration of television editing and special-effects techniques, through the use of classic moments from "Today," "I Love Lucy," "Cheers," "Gilligan's Island," and "Home Improvement."

In a video preview in the queue area, David Letterman and Disney legend Jimmy Macdonald set up the premise of the Monster Sound Show, presented by SONY. This demonstration of film sound-effects techniques features a specially created short film starring Chevy Chase and Martin Short. After the show, in an area called SoundWorks, visitors can enjoy several hands-on sound displays, along with a demonstration of Disney's 3-D binaural sound technology in Soundsations.

Spectacular demonstrations and re-creations of thrilling movie stunts are presented in the Indiana Jones™ Epic Stunt Spectacular, which opened in September 1989. The canopied outdoor amphitheater seats 2,000 guests, who watch a fast-paced stunt show directed by Glenn Randall, who served as stunt coordinator on various films, including *Raiders of the Lost Ark* (1981), *Indiana Jones and the Temple of Doom* (1984), *Poltergeist* (1982), and *Jewel of the Nile* (1985).

*At the entrance to Star Tours, visitors wander through a forest on the Moon of Endor as an Imperial Walker looms over the scene.*

EXPANSION

The first major expansion of the studio was the Back Lot Annex, which opened with the popular Star Tours, presented by Energizer, on December 15, 1989. Star Tours, a flight simulator attraction based on the characters and scenes in the legendary *Star Wars* trilogy, originally opened in Tomorrowland at Disneyland in January 1987. In the Disney-MGM Studios incarnation, however, visitors enter through a gigantic redwood set of the Ewok Village on the Moon of Endor (the village looks terrific at night), complete with an Imperial Walker, in front of the Star Tours sound stage. A rebel X-wing fighter is also on display out front.

Honey, I Shrunk the Kids Movie Set Adventure opened December 17, 1990. Based on the backyard adventure of the 1989 blockbuster *Honey, I Shrunk the Kids*, children may climb and play in an oversized backyard, including giant blocks, an enormous garden hose, and huge spider-web nets. The attraction was designed and fabricated in record time by the Disney Imagineers, who often worked in direct view of the studio visitors.

*The Honey, I Shrunk the Kids Movie Set Adventure provides a gargantuan playground, where visitors can have fun in an oversized "backyard," which includes discarded breakfast cereal.*

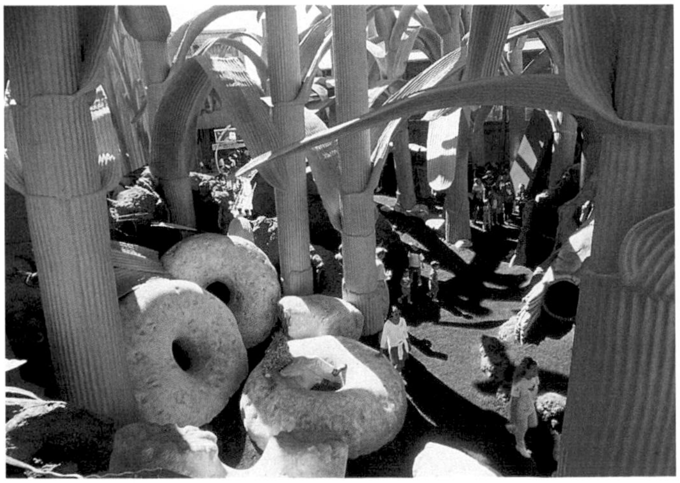

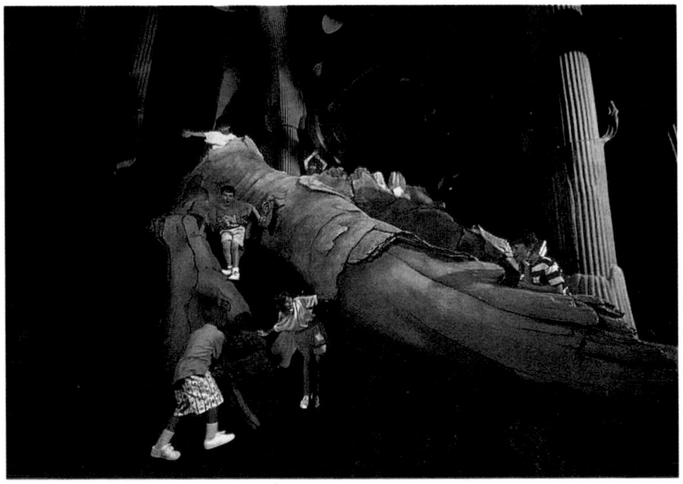

In an aesthetic dictum that dates back to Walt Disney himself, everything about Walt Disney World is meticulously designed and coordinated to create a total environment for visitors. But for more than a decade, the Walt Disney World visitor's first approach to the property was guided by a series of workmanlike road signs. Essentially similar in design to the ubiquitous white-on-green interstate highway signs seen across the country, the original signs at Walt Disney World used plain white type on a brown background.

As the property was developed, Michael Eisner initiated a plan to upgrade, replace, and expand the signage. Largely based on the overwhelming success of their design program for the 1984 Los Angeles Olympic Games, the Los Angeles firm of Sussman/Prezja was invited to propose ideas for the program.

The Sussman/Prezja team's first task was to familiarize themselves with the Walt Disney World property. Realizing the massive scale of the resort, the team divided the property into discrete "districts," which enabled them to eliminate a number of signs. Instead of offering separate signs for every component of the resort, they grouped the signs into categories. In this way, it was possible to replace long, menulike overhead road signs with brief, concise messages.

The team also established a hierarchy of signs, from large highway panels, to secondary message signs, to off-highway directional signs. Color, typography, and form were then explored. After first trying the Disney corporate design typeface, Times Roman, they decided on a heavier, more variable type called Univers, in combination with a typeface called Plantin. The color styling began with Mickey Mouse—black, white, and yellow—then, to these hues, green and purple were added in a playful combination.

In the contour of the signs, shapes and forms were selected in a sort of postmodern configuration, with many using black circles to subtly reference Mickey. Even existing utilitarian stanchions for things like stop, yield, and speed limit signs were replaced with colorful posts and pylons to tie in with the entire program.

In the end, more than 750 signs were created to help visitors find their way throughout Walt Disney World.

TOP: *In the Sci-Fi Dine-In Theater Restaurant, the seating area is a drive-in theater, complete with a fake night sky and twinkling stars.* BOTTOM: *Inside Jim Henson's Muppet*Vision 3D, Kermit the Frog watches as Fozzie Bear gets ready to throw a "pie" at the audience—one of several "3-D tricks."*

With the rapid growth of Disney-MGM Studios, food service facilities had to be added to accommodate the crowds. In the Disney-MGM Studios Commissary, the Imagineers took a basic service facility, the standard studio commissary, and added layers of Hollywood glamour. The stainless steel exterior marquee soars 35 feet into the air. The spectacular entryway features an unusual variety of 10-foot palms. Above the counter a remarkable 50-foot mural, featuring Art Deco interpretations of several Disney-MGM Studios landmarks, is perfectly painted to look like a burnished copper bas-relief. Etched glass panels feature the logos of major Disney businesses, and posters for current Disney releases decorate the dining room. The truly amazing thing about the facility is not just its design, but its construction—the commissary went from design to completion in just seven months.

The Sci-Fi Dine-In Theater Restaurant features an interior architectural style known as atmospheric, used in movie palaces of the 1920s and in Disney's Pirates of the Caribbean. Atmospheric architecture creates the illusion that the visitors are outside, although they are actually indoors. Upon entering, visitors are greeted at the ticket booth maitre d' podium. The seating area is a drive-in theater set, complete with faux night sky and twinkling stars. The tables are designed to look like 1950s convertibles, all facing a giant drive-in screen showing a compilation of cartoons, news clips, drive-in announcements, and trailers from 1950s science fiction B movies. The complimentary appetizer is—what else—popcorn.

Jim Henson's Muppet*Vision 3D premiered May 16, 1991, one year to the day after Jim Henson died. Codeveloped and coproduced by Jim Henson Productions and The Walt Disney Company's Theme Park Productions, the 12-minute film at the core of this attraction was directed by Henson himself. Once the film begins, Kermit the Frog promises that "at no time will we be stooping to any cheap 3-D tricks"—a cue for the cheap gags to fly, as Kermit struggles to maintain order. In the theater, special effects, sound effects, and Audio-Animatronics figures of Bean Bunny, Nicki Napoleon and his Emperor Penguins, Statler and Waldorf, and the Swedish Chef add to the antic action.

The Backlot Theater plays host to a stage show adapted from the current Disney animated feature film. *The Hunchback of Notre Dame* is scheduled to run until June 1997, when *Hercules* is slated to debut.

The Studio Showcase, opened in July 1991, features changing exhibits of sets, props, and costumes from various films and television shows, mainly Walt Disney, Touchstone, and Hollywood Pictures releases, including *Mary Poppins, Who Framed Roger Rabbit, Crimson Tide,* and "Home Improvement."

Dedicated in November 1993, the Academy of Television Arts and Sciences Hall of Fame Plaza is a terraced courtyard sculpture garden devoted to famous performers of the small screen. The centerpiece is the ATAS icon, the Emmy® statue, surrounded by copies of the busts in the forecourt of the ATAS Academy Plaza in North Hollywood, California. The busts honor inductees into the ATAS Television Hall of Fame, including Carol Burnett,

LEFT:
*The Disney animated feature* Beauty and the Beast *is brought to life in a live stage show at Theater of the Stars.*

Jackie Gleason, Mary Tyler Moore, Walter Cronkite, Lucille Ball, Johnny Carson, Walt Disney, Sid Caesar, Milton Berle, Bob Hope, and Alan Alda.

Further expansion of Disney-MGM Studios saw the addition of another famous Hollywood boulevard, Sunset Boulevard, in the summer of 1994. The stepoff from Hollywood Boulevard to Sunset Boulevard is actually the former location of Theater of the Stars, the Disney version of the Hollywood Bowl, which stood from May 1, 1989, to May 2, 1993, adjacent to the Hollywood Brown Derby. The amphitheater was rebuilt alongside Sunset Boulevard and has showcased the popular character show *Beauty and the Beast Live* since its reopening in 1994.

Sunset Boulevard is actually a sparsely occupied corridor leading to the looming Twilight Zone™ Tower of Terror. The street facades are mostly window dressing, but evoke the mood of Hollywood in the 1940s. Once Upon a Time is a boutique in a replica of the distinctive 1926 Spanish-style Carthay Circle Theater in Beverly Hills. The theater is probably best known as the site of the 1937 world premiere of Walt Disney's *Snow White and the Seven Dwarfs.* The original was razed in the 1960s.

Legends of Hollywood was inspired by S. Charles Lee's 1938 Academy Theater, located in Inglewood, California. The distinctive corkscrew spiral tower is emblematic of Lee's flamboyant, soaring style.

Sunset Ranch Market pays homage to the still-famous, still-standing 1934 Farmer's Market on the corner of Third and Fairfax Avenue in Los Angeles. The real Farmer's Market is a few hundred yards away from the former location of the Pan-Pacific Auditorium (replicated at the park entry gate).

The Twilight Zone™ Tower of Terror opened on July 22, 1994. The foreboding 199-foot tower is the tallest attraction on the entire Walt Disney World property and projects a properly terrifying mood (when one of the frequent Florida thunderstorms rolls in, the effect is positively cinematic). The Hollywood Tower Hotel, you see, was the site of a supernatural disaster. According to legend, on Halloween night, 1939, lightning struck the popular Hollywood landmark. An entire guest wing vanished, along with an elevator carrying five people. The disappearance has remained a mystery, and the ven-

*Sunset Boulevard is the "theater district" of Disney-MGM Studios with replicas of memorable moviehouses, including the 1926 Carthay Circle Theater in Beverly Hills* (TOP).

The
HOLLYWOOD TOWER
Hot'l

*The lobby of The Hollywood Tower Hotel appears to be forever frozen in 1939.*

OPPOSITE:
*Looming 199 feet high, the Twilight Zone Tower of Terror is the tallest attraction on the entire Walt Disney World property.*

erable hotel, rumored to be haunted, has stood deserted and decaying for more than 50 years. Visitors enter through the once-grand lobby, and in a musty library Rod Serling appears on a television monitor, inviting guests to take an elevator ride—into The Twilight Zone. The elevator ride culminates in two heart-stopping 130-foot free-fall drops, with a rocketlike ascent in between. The Hollywood Tower Hotel contains some of the most realistic and detailed set dressing in the history of Imagineering. The ambiance that has been created within the hotel setting is just as worthy of visitor attention as the final plunge.

Also added during the 1994 expansion is the Studio Tips Board, an information kiosk that leads visitors to the shortest lines and potentially overlooked events and attractions. Adjacent to the Tips Board is a miniature replica of the Mulholland Fountain at Riverside Drive and Los Feliz Boulevard. The original was built to honor William Mulholland, who masterminded the import of water from the Owens River in the Sierra Nevada by viaduct to Los Angeles.

The American Film Institute Showcase joined Disney-MGM Studios in 1996. The permanent exhibit highlights the careers of AFI's 24 Life Achievement Award winners, including Steven Spielberg, Jack Nicholson, Elizabeth Taylor, Orson Welles, James Cagney, Bette Davis, and Clint Eastwood. In addition, the exhibit highlights film preservation and the effort to save films in danger of being lost forever, as well as the many disciplines involved behind the scenes in film production.

This exhibit, like so much of Disney-MGM Studios, portrays the myths of Hollywood more cohesively than Hollywood itself. In 1990 in the *Los Angeles Times,* Sam Hall Kaplan published an appreciation of the "Hollywood that never was—and always will be" at Disney-MGM Studios:

> *You would think that by now the value of historic preservation in economic and social terms (read tourism and pride) would be appreciated in Tinseltown, the dream factory of the world. It is certainly being appreciated here in the Florida outback.*
>
> *So, while Los Angeles is letting its landmarks deteriorate or be bulldozed, Disney, after a fashion, is saving them. . . . Perhaps someday to get a sense of the rich cultural and architectural heritage of Hollywood in the '30s, we may just have to travel to Florida and pay an entrance fee.*

Silver Creek Falls
WILDERNESS
LODGE
Urban Design Gro

# CHAPTER SIX

# THE REST OF THE "WORLD"

*In my view, wholesome pleasure, sport, and recreation are as vital to this nation as productive work.*

—WALT DISNEY

OPPOSITE:
*Concept paintings for the rest of the "World" (clockwise from top left): Dixie Landings Resort, Wilderness Lodge, Typhoon Lagoon, Old Key West Resort, Celebration, Blizzard Beach. Center: The Adventurers Club on Pleasure Island.*

During its first 25 years Walt Disney World grew up. In 1971 a visitor could expect accommodations at a unique hotel, a day or two at the Magic Kingdom, some nice meals, a game of tennis, a round of golf, and some shopping. In the ensuing 25 years the explosion of resort activities at Walt Disney World has ensured that a visitor can *regularly* vacation at Walt Disney World without threat of boredom—indeed, without even duplicating the same activities and experiences.

The development of resort amenities began with golf, boating, camping, and tennis. A few years later shopping was added to the list as the quiet Lake Buena Vista Village opened on March 22, 1975. In 1977 the *Empress Lilly,* a riverboat-themed restaurant-lounge, opened with three restaurants—the Fisherman's Deck, the Steerman's Quarters, and the Empress Room. It featured the most elegant dining on Walt Disney World property. (The *Empress Lilly,* which became part of Pleasure Island in 1989, was closed for renovation in 1995 and reopened with Fulton's Crab House as its restaurant passenger in March 1996.)

### DISNEY VILLAGE MARKETPLACE

The shopping village was later christened Walt Disney World Village and then Disney Village Marketplace. Today, thanks to a massive renovation project, Disney Village Marketplace has the vibrant feel of a festive village. The grounds and facilities have been remodeled; walkways have been broadened; gardens and outdoor seating areas have been added. Topiary figures and performing fountains add to the inviting ambiance. Eighteen shops, a half-

*Located along Buena Vista Lagoon* (TOP), *Disney Village Marketplace features "Disney touches" like topiary figures and performing fountains* (RIGHT). *Disney artwork is the main attraction at the appropriately named Art of Disney at Disney Village Marketplace* (ABOVE).

dozen restaurants, and a variety of resort activities are all part of Disney Village Marketplace.

PLEASURE ISLAND

As part of the construction boom that included Disney-MGM Studios, the Wonders of Life, the EPCOT Resorts, and Disney's Caribbean Beach Resort, plans for a nightlife district called Pleasure Island were unveiled. (This is not the island in Disney's *Pinocchio* [1940] where little boys drank beer, smoked cigars, shot pool, and turned into jackasses.)

The new waterfront entertainment center answered a recognized need for more evening activities for adult vacationers, conventioneers, and local residents. For years, the Walt Disney World property had been a relatively sleepy place after about 9 P.M., and visitors in search of a nightclub, dancing, live music, a late supper, or the latest movie had to drive into downtown Orlando.

Plans for Pleasure Island were revealed by Michael Eisner on July 21, 1986, in a press conference aboard the *Empress Lilly.* Construction began in August 1986, and the complex opened in May 1989. Located on a 6-acre island on the 35-acre Buena Vista Lagoon and connected to the mainland by footbridges, Pleasure Island featured six innovative themed nightclubs (a seventh was added in 1992) and a number of imaginative merchandise shops and specialty food outlets.

*A riverboat with a themed restaurant-lounge, the* Empress Lilly *is named after Walt Disney's widow, Lillian Bounds Disney.*

**OPPOSITE:**
*Easily reachable by footbridge, Pleasure Island offers Walt Disney World visitors nighttime entertainment with seven themed nightclubs and a variety of intriguing shops and specialty food outlets.*

THE STORY OF PLEASURE ISLAND

The concept for Pleasure Island relied on one of Disney's greatest skills: storytelling. One of the first efforts of the Imagineering team was to develop a background story, or mythology, for the island:

*In the late 19th century, an adventuresome Pittsburgh entrepreneur, Merriweather Adam Pleasure, moved to the island and founded a canvas manufacturing and sail fabricating industry. The Florida climate favored his business, and though the merchant sailing industry was in its twilight, pleasure yachting discovered his superior product and his success was made.*

*The earliest buildings on the island were a wood-burning power generating plant (collapsed and rebuilt in concrete in 1934), the textile mill where high-grade canvas duck was woven, the circular fabrication building where sail making was done, and the owner's residence. During the First World War, the manufacture of military tents required several additions to the mill and fabrication buildings. After the war, the pleasure craft industry expanded and boathouses for yacht outfitting were added. Before the catastrophic decline of the St. John's aquifer in 1928, yachting clientele were accommodated in a salubrious club. Pleasure commissioned the building after becoming acquainted with the work of the Messrs. Sir Edwin Lutyens, Charles MacIntosh and Eliel Saarinen during a visit to the Paris ateliers of the Ecole des Beaux Arts.*

*Demand for the outfitting of luxury watercraft ebbed during the Depression, and although financially unscathed in the market crash of 1929, the founder of Pleasure Canvas and Sailmaking, Inc., left the business in the hands of his two sons and embarked on a late-in-life adventure to the far reaches of the earth. Aware of the westering circumnavigations of Irving Johnson and the youthful crews of his "Yankee Clipper," Merriweather Pleasure commissioned the yacht "Domino" (named for his then-favorite pastime), which brilliantly foresaw the awesome J-boat formula. With his daughter Merriam and her second husband, he embarked on a series of eastward 'round-the-world voyages. They returned from their many expeditions with a vast treasure of adventure and discovery. The trophies eventually overwhelmed Pleasure's comfortable Bermuda-style house, and he built a warehouse to store and catalog them.*

*In 1937, Pleasure hit upon a novel advancement in amphibious aviation, and became consumed with the development of a secret device. He worked feverishly with a small staff of experts in a mysterious metal building he constructed just offshore in Lake Buena Vista.*

*The "Domino" was presumably lost with Merriweather, Merriam, and all hands, having been reported pitchpoled in a howling summer storm while attempting a circumnavigation of Antarctica in December 1941.*

*With the outbreak of World War II, Henry and Stewart Pleasure's sail and canvas business boomed, so much so that they added several large prefabricated steel buildings to house their expanded operations. The success continued after the war into the 1950s, sail making and chandlery being augmented by a flying boat service, until Stewart's poor business decisions and Henry's lavish lifestyle forced Pleasure Canvas and Sailmaking, Inc., into bankruptcy in 1955. As a note of finality, Hurricane Connie inflicted near-total destruction two weeks before the creditors' sale, ripping the roof and siding off the 1937 amphibian building and leaving the island an unsaleable shambles.*

ABOVE:
*At Mannequins Dance Palace even the dance floor is in motion, revolving past dynamic displays of fashion figures.*

RIGHT:
*Guests enjoy live music outdoors at the West End Stage, at the west end of Pleasure Island.*

## THE PLEASURES OF PLEASURE ISLAND

The newly constructed buildings were created to appear organic, as if Disney Imagineers had restored the waterfront as a nightlife attraction on the ruins of this former enterprise.

Pleasure's engine factory, with a large rotating assembly floor, was converted into Mannequins Dance Palace, a cutting-edge dance music club, similar to those found in New York and West Hollywood. In Mannequins, elaborately wardrobed fashion figures populate dynamic sets, surrounding the revolving 42-foot-diameter dance floor.

In the Adventurers Club the testosterone-laden atmosphere of world exploration and colonialism circa 1850 to 1939 is re-created. Unusual, fantastic, and eccentric memorabilia from around the world (acquired by Pleasure on expedition or contributed by international club members) cover the walls, hallways, and rooms of the club. A giant stone face, known as Miss Zenobia, tells fortunes and spins tales from the past, while ghostly apparitions sit beside visitors at the Illusions Bar. The peculiar members and staff of the Adventurers Club provide live entertainment.

One of Mr. Pleasure's cavernous warehouses, which once stored the treasures of world expeditions, is now the storage facility for giggles, chortles, and guffaws—stand-up comedians and improvisational comedy acts appear onstage at the Comedy Warehouse.

Pleasure's huge greenhouse became the Neon Armadillo Music Saloon, with country music in an American Southwest setting. Disney's television subsidiary, Buena Vista Television, even developed a (short-lived) syndicated country music television variety series, "Countdown at the Neon Armadillo," which was taped here and aired from September to December 1993.

The Fireworks Factory was once Mr. Pleasure's own fireworks-making facility. Inside, tables and chairs have been arranged around blackened metal siding and blown-out brick walls. The restaurant features authentic American barbecue selections cooked over wood coals.

Portobello Yacht Club is housed in Pleasure's former residence, a stately Bermuda-style home featuring elegantly appointed pastel-toned rooms with a nautical decor. Portobello specializes in wood-burning-oven pizzas, homemade pastas, fresh seafood, and authentic northern Italian cuisine. For a different experience, diners may now board the *Empress Lilly* and enjoy the seafood fare of Fulton's Crab House.

Several changes have occurred since opening day in 1989. The XZFR Rockin' Rollerdrome originally featured a central dance floor surrounded by a second-level roller-skating rink and had a DJ in a booth suspended from the ceiling. The roller skating was a novelty—and a little too dangerous—so the facility was re-themed to become the Rock & Roll Beach Club. The second and third floors now contain billiard tables and other games, and live bands perform hits from the 1950s to the present.

TOP: *The Adventurers Club is filled with eccentric memorabilia.* CENTER: *Stand-up comedians and improvisational comedy acts take the stage at the Comedy Warehouse.* BOTTOM: *At the Neon Armadillo Music Saloon, country music is the featured act.*

## PORT ORLEANS AND DIXIE LANDINGS

The antebellum South along the Mississippi is skillfully evoked in the second moderate-rate Walt Disney World resort area, encompassing Port Orleans and Dixie Landings. These themed resorts (totaling 3,056 rooms) are connected by a winding road and picturesque waterways, to capture the mystery and romance of a trip up the Mississippi River from New Orleans to Natchez. (In Walt Disney World geography, resort guests can travel by flat-bottomed boats even farther downriver, to the shops and showplaces of the Disney Village Marketplace and Pleasure Island.)

Disney's Port Orleans and Disney's Dixie Landings are actually two distinct resort hotels of different size and character that share a major theme. They both pay homage to the river, which links them, and they both offer the same type of accommodations and amenities, but provide subtly different "southern" experiences.

At the southern end of the site, where the river is widest, the 1,008-room Port Orleans opened in May 1991. Port Orleans evokes the sophisticated, urban river South. Emanating from the public square, pedestrian streets lead down rows of guest room buildings—all in the style of the French Quarter, bedecked with balconies and wrought-iron railings in a variety of sizes, styles, colors, and materials.

Port Orleans features one restaurant, a food court, a lounge, and a poolside bar. In addition, there is a shop, a themed swimming pool, croquet, and boat and bike rental facilities.

The second resort (2,048 rooms, which opened beginning in February 1992) suggests, by contrast, the plantation South. If the first resort seems a city, the second resembles a town, depicting the rustic lifestyle of the Old South. More dispersed than Port Orleans, Dixie Landings is built as a series of bayou villages and great plantation homes, which all exhibit the distinct character of the upriver South.

Four three-story antebellum mansions, each housing 256 guest rooms, overlook lawns and tree-lined alleys and fields of crops toward the river. Bayou Parish is a series of rustic, cracker-style villages tucked into and spread out among the pine forests and organized around a series of three creeks and paths. The 16 two-story, 64-unit buildings have a distinctive architectural style that comes from the deep wood South.

Dixie Landings has a restaurant, food court, lounge, general store, and game room, as well as five swimming pools and fishing facilities.

Winding paths lead to the focal point of the plantation, Ol' Man Island, a three-and-a-half-acre recreation complex with pools, spa, fishing hole, and playground. Bicycles and boats are available at Dixie Levee.

*Port Orleans*

*Dixie Landings, Magnolia Bend*

## WILDERNESS LODGE

Disney's Wilderness Lodge Resort, which opened in May 1994, is based on a romantic vision of the early West, combined with an interpretation of the National Park Service lodges created between 1904 and 1924 under the direction of Stephen Mather. Inspired by the Arts and Crafts movement, the lodges of this period architecturally unified the romantic elements of the unspoiled wilderness parks—harmony with nature, closeness to wildlife, the mysticism of Native American culture—into a rustic and uniquely American cultural style.

The 729-room Wilderness Lodge Resort, reminiscent of the Old Faithful Inn in Yellowstone, is hidden away on the shores of Bay Lake, surrounded by towering pine and oak groves, with liberal use of birch, pine, and cedar trees to create the feeling of a Western forest. The lodge building is eight stories tall and features extensive use of quarried stone and authentic lodgepole pine.

The soaring, log-structured main lobby is the centerpiece of Wilderness Lodge. Massive, six-story bundled log columns help support roof dormers that bathe the multicolored floor tiles below in natural light. Two 55-foot totem poles—the eagle and the raven—carved in Washington State, bracket the lobby.

The towering centerpiece of the lodge is a massive, 82-foot-tall, three-walled stone fireplace. Colorful rock layers, reflecting the strata of the Grand Canyon and two billion years of history, are captured in the structure of the fireplace. There are even fossilized remains of prehistoric animals and plants.

Four massive chandeliers with torch-cut rustic scenes, topped with glowing teepees, grace the lobby's center. Tucked throughout the lobby are porches and reading areas, and additional intimate spaces are left for visitors to discover within the six-story guest wings.

A bubbling hot spring in the main lobby expands into a rocky geothermal area outside the building. The water flows under a picturesque window wall to become Silver Creek in the upper courtyard. The quiet, contemplative creek widens and is transformed into a rushing, roaring waterfall, which plummets past Overlook Point, another traditional National Park icon, and widens again into the swimming area. A kids' pool and hot and cold spas augment the swimming area, which seems to flow into Bay Lake.

The majestic setting of Wilderness Lodge is complemented by themed dining experiences which include Artist Point Restaurant, Territory Lounge, Whispering Canyon Cafe, and Roaring Forks. The resort also features a child-care center, a retail shop, an arcade, and a poolside bar.

ABOVE:
*Fireworks, special-effects lighting, and confetti celebrate each night at Pleasure Island.*

ABOVE RIGHT:
*Opened in 1994, Pleasure Island Jazz Company recalls jazz clubs of the 1930s, with live jazz music.*

Videopolis East was modeled after the then-hot dance venue at Disneyland in Anaheim (since closed). Appealing to the under-21 set, Videopolis was a nonalcoholic nightclub with 170 video monitors featuring the latest rock videos. Videopolis was quickly converted to a progressive club called Cage. Today, the retro '70s club 8TRAX occupies the space.

The food court at Merriweather's Market proved disappointing, and it was closed and completely renovated to become Pleasure Island Jazz Company, reminiscent of jazz clubs of the 1930s, with live music daily.

The West End Stage, an outdoor venue for live performances, was added shortly after the island opened; it is located (suitably enough) at the west end of the island. Every night, Pleasure Island celebrates New Year's Eve with fireworks, special-effects lighting, and confetti by the ton.

Across the footbridge from the central island, visitors can take in the latest movies at the AMC Pleasure Island 10. The theaters have high-quality projection systems and six-track THX stereo surround sound—even computer-calculated sight lines. Walt Disney Imagineering, working from original plans developed by AMC, designed the exterior of the theater to tie in with the restored waterfront theme of Pleasure Island. By late 1996 AMC will have 14 new screens, making the AMC Pleasure Island 24 the largest movie theater in all of Florida.

In December 1994 Planet Hollywood, the international restaurant chain partly owned by actors Sylvester Stallone, Arnold Schwarzenegger, Bruce Willis, and Demi Moore, opened with a gala event. The sphere-shaped building is 95 feet tall and "floats" on Village Lake, between the AMC Pleasure Island movie theaters and Pleasure Island. To achieve this effect, water was drained from the area of construction. Two hundred steel pilings were pounded into the ground to establish a solid foundation, and a concrete slab was poured on top of that. The rest of the restaurant was completely built and water-sealed before water was returned to the lagoon

*The spherical, 95-foot-high Planet Hollywood "floats" on Village Lake behind a shop full of Planet Hollywood merchandise.*

around it. Inside is a treasure trove of movie memorabilia: props, costumes, and models housed in wall cases or hung from the ceiling. There is even a full-size Herbie (*The Love Bug*) Volkswagen suspended high above the floor.

Two celebrity nightclubs, a 1,500-seat performing arts theater, two star-name restaurants, and two Disney superstores will double the size of Pleasure Island and Disney Village Marketplace by 1997. A new name for the expanded area encompassing both old and new is pending. The latest projects include:

House of Blues—Inspired by one of America's most celebrated musical traditions, House of Blues will feature a 1,500-person capacity restaurant/music venue that will house a television production facility, multimedia development site, and radio broadcasting center. The music hall will highlight an array of live music seven nights a week, and the restaurant will feature eclectic Delta-inspired cuisine. The concept was conceived by entrepreneur Isaac Tigrett in association with actor Dan Aykroyd.

Wolfgang Puck's Cafe—The world-famous chef will build his first restaurant in Florida here, featuring his innovative California cuisine in a casual setting.

Lario's—This restaurant/nightclub created by Latina superstar Gloria Estefan and her husband, Emilio, brings the sizzle of Miami's South Beach to Disney. Like its popular sister restaurant, the Lario's at Walt Disney World will feature the flavors and rhythms of Cuba.

Disney's Entertainment Theater—This performing arts theater will feature Walt Disney World performances and visiting entertainers.

The World of Disney and Team Mickey Superstore—This 50,000-square-foot multistory building will include two new Disney mega-markets. The World of Disney will be the largest character merchandise shopping emporium in the world. Team Mickey will be national headquarters for merchandise and information about Disney sports franchises and events.

*This tabletop model guided the Imagineers in creating Typhoon Lagoon, a topsy-turvy water recreation area.*

BOTTOM:
Miss Tilly, *a shrimp boat caught in the mythical typhoon, was left teetering atop the lagoon's volcano, Mount Mayday.*

OPPOSITE:
*The overwhelming success of Typhoon Lagoon led to the creation of another water park, Blizzard Beach, allegedly created by a freak winter storm. On the face of Mount Gushmore* (TOP), *"former" ski slalom courses and bobsled and sledding runs have become downhill water slides* (BOTTOM). *The ski jump is the tallest and fastest water slide in the world.*

## TYPHOON LAGOON

The mythical Hurricane Connie that demolished Pleasure Island wreaked its fictional havoc across Buena Vista Drive as well and created the topsy-turvy environment of Typhoon Lagoon. The huge wave of wind and water left nothing in the little tropical village untouched. Surfboards were embedded in trees. Parts of boats and buoys dangled in thatched roofs. *Miss Tilly,* a small shrimp boat caught in the typhoon, was left precariously perched atop the pinnacle of the lagoon's resident volcano, Mount Mayday.

*A furious storm once roared 'cross the sea,*
*catching ships in its path, helpless to flee.*
*Instead of a certain and watery doom,*
*the winds swept them here to Typhoon Lagoon.*

Construction of Typhoon Lagoon was part of the late 1980s expansion boom. Plans for this giant themed water recreation area were unveiled by Michael Eisner at ground-breaking ceremonies on February 4, 1987. Construction began the same month, and the park opened on June 1, 1989.

Typhoon Lagoon is a 34-acre water entertainment complex with the largest man-made watershed mountain in the world and pools for snorkeling, surfing, swimming, floating, and sliding. Located halfway between Walt Disney World Village and Disney-MGM Studios, Typhoon Lagoon includes a 95-foot-high mountain with nine water slides and roaring streams up to 400 feet long, a 2.5-acre wave-making lagoon, and a saltwater snorkeling pool, where guests come face to face with colorful creatures of the Caribbean, including snapper, angelfish, groupers, parrotfish, and sharks.

No one could have predicted the overwhelming success of Typhoon Lagoon. Shortly after its grand opening, Typhoon Lagoon, like River Country before it, was turning visitors away early in the morning because the park was already full to capacity. The Imagineers immediately put a third water park on the drawing boards.

BLIZZARD BEACH

Rather than repeat the themes established in River Country or Typhoon Lagoon, the Imagineers came up with a completely crazy new concept—and a new mythology. As legend has it, Blizzard Beach was created by a freak winter storm, which dropped snow over the western side of the Walt Disney World property. Florida's first snow-ski resort was planned—but rather short-lived. Temperatures soared, and the ice and snow rapidly began to melt. Dismayed ski resort operators, ready to close, spotted a playful alligator sliding down the liquid ice slopes and realized the melting snow created the tallest, fastest, and most exhilarating water-filled ski and toboggan runs in the world. As a result, the ski resort/water adventure park was born. Former ski slalom courses and bobsled and sledding runs became downhill water slides. The chairlift could still carry swimmers to the top of the slides. The ski jump became the world's tallest and fastest water slide. The melting snow revealed welcoming beaches, a preteen play area, and many other activities.

Appropriately, the all-new 66-acre Blizzard Beach water adventure park opened on April Fool's Day in 1995. Now, whether by bobsledding down the snowy slopes of Mount Gushmore or plunging straight down Summit Plummet at 55 miles per hour, Walt Disney World guests get all the thrills of a northern ski resort—but Blizzard Beach is strictly tropical, and the ice is limited to what's floating in the soft drinks.

*Becoming a member of the Disney Vacation Club entitles vacationers to stay in this Key West–styled resort at Walt Disney World.*

DISNEY VACATION CLUB

Another first-of-its-kind Disney project debuted in October 1991 with the launch of Disney Vacation Club (DVC), a flexible vacation concept that offers an array of exciting vacation experiences.

The collection of Disney Vacation Club Resorts includes the flagship Disney Vacation Club Resort located off Community Drive at Bonnet Creek Parkway, adjacent to the Lake Buena Vista Golf Course. The resort features 497 spacious studio, one-, two-, and three-bedroom homes designed in a Key West theme. The studios include a mini-kitchen and all other vacation homes have a fully equipped kitchen, a TV/VCR, and a master suite with a whirlpool tub. (This original site changed its name to Disney's Old Key West Resort in early 1996 with the addition of Disney's Boardwalk Villas also at Walt Disney World.)

Vero Beach, Florida, became the site of the second Disney Vacation Club Resort, the first Disney resort built separately from a Disney theme park. Disney's Hilton Head Island Resort in South Carolina opened March 1, 1996. Within walking distance of Epcot, Disney's Boardwalk Villas (the fourth Disney Vacation Club Resort) opened June 30, 1996. This waterfront resort captures the essence of the magnificent Atlantic Seaboard of the 1930s. Resort amenities include a health club, poolside arcade, tennis courts, and a themed pool.

A NEW TEAM IN PLACE

During this period of enormous expansion (and the 20th anniversary of Walt Disney World) in 1991, several senior-management changes were made. Michael Eisner and Frank Wells named Judson Green president of Walt Disney Attractions. Green brought the vital experience of a decade with Disney to bear in taking over the day-to-day operation of Disneyland and Walt Disney World. He had joined Walt Disney World as manager of management audit in 1981. Green had moved to the Euro Disney project in 1987, as senior vice president and chief financial officer, and in 1989 he had been named senior vice president and CFO for The Walt Disney Company.

Green, along with Dick Nunis (who was simultaneously promoted to chairman of Walt Disney Attractions), promised to see through the myriad upcoming projects at Walt Disney World with a sure hand.

THE DISNEY INSTITUTE

The opening of The Disney Institute in February 1996 brought a unique type of vacation to Walt Disney World. Now there is a special vacation resort for adults—couples, singles, empty-nesters—as well as for families with children over 7 years old.

It is a place where guests can engage their bodies, excite their minds, and expand their horizons through a variety of entertaining and enriching

## "THE MAGIC LINKDOM?" WALT DISNEY WORLD, OF COURSE!

It is a small population, to be sure, that thinks immediately of *golf* when Walt Disney World is mentioned—but the connection is not nearly as tenuous or strange as it might seem to the uninitiated.

Golf was a part of the initial development of Walt Disney World. When the vacation kingdom first opened in 1971, it opened with two courses, the Palm and the Magnolia.

Designed by Joe Lee, the Palm has been ranked among the nation's top 75 resort courses by *Golf Digest*. The course, with wooded fairways and nine water hazards, plays 5,398 yards from the front tees, 6,461 from the middle, and 6,957 from the back. Also designed by Lee, the Magnolia is a tree-dotted 5,232 yards from the front tees, 6,642 from the middle, and 7,190 from the back. The Magnolia and the Palm share a pair of driving ranges and putting greens.

A nine-hole family-play course, Oak Trail, is also located adjacent to the Magnolia course, near the Polynesian Resort. This 2,913-yard layout with a par of 36 is designed with the beginner in mind.

The Lake Buena Vista course followed with the development of Lake Buena Vista Village (now Disney Village and The Disney Institute) in 1974. Also designed by Joe Lee, this course measures 5,176 yards from the front tees, 6,268 from the middle, and 6,829 from the back. The course also has a driving range and putting green. Together with the Palm and the Magnolia, the Lake Buena Vista hosts about 400 tournaments a year, including the annual Walt Disney World/Oldsmobile Golf Classic.

In 1991 the Magic Linkdom grew to 99 holes of golf with the addition of the Osprey Ridge and Eagle Pines courses. Located in the northeastern part of the Walt Disney World property, the courses share the Bonnet Lake Golf Club clubhouse, a driving range, and a putting green.

Osprey Ridge, designed by Tom Fazio, features high mounding and natural framing. The par-72 layout plays 5,402 yards from the forward tees, 6,680 yards from the middle, and 7,101 yards from the back.

Contrasting with Osprey Ridge is the Pete Dye–designed Eagle Pines. Distinctive with its low, dished fairways and pine straw instead of rough, the par-72 course plays 4,838 yards from the front tees, 6,309 yards from the middle, and 6,772 from the pro tees.

The new planned community at Walt Disney World, Celebration, will feature an 18-hole, par-72 course by renowned father-and-son course architects Robert Trent Jones, Sr. and Robert Trent Jones, Jr. A three-hole junior course, exclusively for children and adults with children, is part of the design.

## ALL-STAR RESORTS

The overwhelming success of the moderate-priced Caribbean Beach, Dixie Landings, and Port Orleans resorts inspired Disney to enter into the fast-growing economy hotel market. The economy-priced All-Star Resorts are located among pristine forests on a 246-acre site at the northwest quadrant of the World Drive and Highway 192 interchange. The resort complex incorporates colorful, distinctive Pop Art icon elements from sports and music themes within its unique exterior facades.

The 3,840-room complex was designed in two phases, with each phase containing a separate, uniquely themed hotel of 1,920 rooms in 10 units. The first phase, Disney's All-Star Sports Resort, opened in spring 1994. It represents five themes—football, baseball, basketball, tennis, and surfing. Among the giant icons are sharkfins, whistles, megaphones, footballs, and basketballs.

The first unit of the resort's second phase, the All-Star Music Resort—with Broadway, country, jazz, rock, and calypso music themes—opened in fall 1994. Here guests discover a three-story pair of cowboy boots, trombone player silhouettes on the roof line, a huge walk-through neon-lit jukebox, and a giant Broadway theater marquee.

Guests arriving at Disney's All-Star Resorts first visit one of the two commercial centers—Stadium Hall or Melody Hall—to check in. Each reception area is filled with memorabilia to introduce the resort themes. Large stars, graphic drawings, and bright colors set the mood, and each hall houses the front desk, guest services, luggage shuttle service, merchandise shop, and arcade. Here, guests can also enjoy a variety of dining experiences in the End Zone and Intermission Food Courts. These 500-seat food courts are decorated with various memorable articles reflecting the different sports and music.

Uniquely themed swimming pools are located in both parts of the complex. At Disney's All-Star Sports Resort, the featured pool has a tropical surfing setting surrounded by 12 surfboards, with two 38-foot-high shark fins circling the pool. Disney's All-Star Music Resort offers a tropical island setting and a giant guitar-shaped pool. Another pool resembles a piano top, with a keyboard deck and a huge transistor radio nearby.

At Disney's All-Star Resorts, the designers have taken basic motel components, and elevated the guest experience to a Disney level through the focused attention on design, graphics, and decor.

programs. In a fun, creatively charged atmosphere, guests may, among other things, animate a film, whip up a soufflé, direct a TV show, or scale a rock wall. There are more than 60 program offerings from which to choose.

The Disney Institute is a tranquil lakeside enclave on the reconstructed site of the Disney Village Resort. Smaller in scale than other Disney resorts—with only 457 rooms—it offers guests an intimate, personalized vacation experience. The architecture is reminiscent of a small town, and the facilities include a welcome center, a broadcast-quality performance hall, 28 studios and workshops, a sports and fitness center with a full-service spa, an 18-hole championship golf course, lighted outdoor clay tennis courts, an outdoor amphitheater, six outdoor swimming pools, a cinema, and a youth center.

Through the past decade, Michael Eisner and his team have taken projects and ideas that Disney has never before attempted, identified quintessentially "Disney" characteristics, and created a natural evolution in the established and well-known Disney culture. The Disney Institute is one of the finest examples of this skill. It represents an elevation of the philosophical ideals perceived by most people in the definition of Disney. The inspiration for The Disney Institute came from Michael Eisner himself, by way of his wife, Jane.

More than 100 years ago a group of Methodist ministers in upstate New York created a school, the Chautauqua Institution, to train their Sunday school teachers. Over the century Chautauqua evolved into a small community that hosts an annual summer cultural arts festival. The nine-week festival presents a variety of events, from operas to modern dance exhibitions, musical plays to science lectures. There are activities for children, ranging from arts and crafts to sports and fitness. Both guests and residents are encouraged to observe rehearsals as well as performances, to discuss ideas with guest lecturers throughout the day, and simply to relax within the peaceful environment.

When Jane Eisner took Michael to visit Chautauqua in 1985, he was immediately inspired by its blend of enrichment, education, and fun. The visit led him to believe that The Walt Disney Company might indeed be able to provide just such an environment for its guests. Following his Chautauqua visit, Michael Eisner wrote to Frank Wells: "If Henry Adams was right when he said 'a teacher influences eternity,' then Walt Disney World may still need that gated attraction that teaches and improves the quality of life in the Disney fashion."

Several years of concept testing and market research followed, which refined the notion of a Disney vacation destination, offering a combination of enrichment and enjoyment in a relaxed atmosphere—Chautauqua-inspired but quintessentially Disney.

The Disney Institute feels like a community, as guests walk or bike to and from their rooms, the dining hall, and program activities. With a guest-to-instructor ratio of approximately 15 to 1, The Disney Institute offers a genuine personalization of the guest experience, something that is simply

TOP:
*Clustered near a quiet lake, the buildings of the Disney Institute suggest a small town.*

BOTTOM:
*Guests may choose from more than 60 activities, including cooking.*

not possible in the parks, given the volume of visitors. The programs are both fun and significant, emphasizing understanding by doing. At the end of their stay, visitors will leave the institute with knowledge that they can apply to their daily lives.

*Residential streets in Celebration blend apartments, townhouses, single-family, and custom houses in the same neighborhood—unlike most planned communities, where different housing types are developed in separate zones.*

### CELEBRATION

One of the most recent projects at Walt Disney World actually brings the Florida project full circle, fulfilling the desires and aspirations of Walt Disney himself. Celebration is the project, a planned community much in the spirit of the EPCOT that Walt Disney envisioned.

Celebration promises to be a true planned city, including a downtown area, health center, school, teaching academy, bank, post office, town hall, recreational facilities, and housing. Under the direction of the Celebration Company, a subsidiary of The Walt Disney Company, the master plan architects are Cooper, Robertson & Partners and Robert A. M. Stern Architects.

Celebration is located in the southern sector of the Walt Disney World property in northwest Osceola County, south of U.S. Highway 192 along Interstate Highway 4. The town site itself is 4,900 acres, surrounded by a protected greenbelt of 4,700 acres. The diverse housing options will include apartments, townhouses, and single-family homes, with 8,000 potential housing units and a potential population of 20,000. Celebration's amenities will include an 18-hole public golf course, a public school, a teaching academy, offices, a health facility, cinemas, walking paths, nature trails, village parks, and a downtown lake.

The Celebration Company is the owner and developer, maintaining ownership of the downtown, golf course, and office park, with a projected total buildout investment of $2.5 billion. Home buyers will own their homes and land. Celebration will be an unincorporated town within the jurisdiction of Osceola County. Two Community Development Districts (Enterprise and Celebration CDDs) will provide funding for the infrastructure of Celebration, and two community associations will manage the neighborhoods. The completion of Celebration may take 15 years.

A variety of businesses and civic institutions will establish downtown Celebration as a place to work, shop, and socialize. Plans include an inn designed by Graham Gund, a town hall designed by Philip Johnson, a post office designed by Michael Graves, a bank designed by Venturi, Scott Brown & Associates, a cinema, a bookstore, shops designed by Cesar Pellí, and restaurants. Much of the downtown area will adjoin a promenade circling a lake.

In 1966 Walt Disney said, ". . . we're counting on the cooperation of American industry to provide their very best thinking during the planning and creation of our Experimental Prototype Community of Tomorrow. And most important of all: when EPCOT has become a reality, and we find the need for technologies that don't even exist today, it is our hope that EPCOT will stimulate American industry to develop new solutions that will meet the needs of people expressed right here in this experimental community."

*A quiet lake lends its charm to the downtown area of Celebration.*

In 1996 this philosophy of eliciting, developing, and ultimately displaying the best ideas available is a primary component of the Celebration project. The infrastructure of Celebration has been developed in cooperation with the state of Florida and the Osceola County government. Corporate and industrial strategic alliances are being explored with a variety of important companies.

Florida Hospital will be the owner and operator of a 65-acre state-of-the-art health campus, called Celebration Health. Primary health care, including dentistry, will be available at Celebration Health. A state-of-the-art fitness center will offer classes and activities for the entire family. At the Center for Health Innovations, research, training, and demonstration of new technologies will be the focus.

Designed by Italian architect Aldo Rossi, phase one of Celebration Place has already been completed. Celebration Place is part of a 109-acre commercial center, which may ultimately include more than a million square feet of office space. Phase one is 240,000 square feet and is home to employees of Disney Development Company (now Walt Disney Imagineering), Disney Vacation Club, Disney Cruise Line, and other third-party tenants. It is hoped that prominent companies expanding into or relocating to central Florida will join these business residents of Celebration.

The name of the community sums up its lively spirit. "We looked at what made communities great in our past, added what we've learned from the best practices today, and combined this with vision and hope for strong communities in the future," Michael Eisner said in 1995. "At Disney, we are constantly reminding ourselves the real magic is not in buildings, physical structures, or even technology. We are as interested in the civic infrastructure as the physical infrastructure, because it is the human element that will make the community great."

# WALT DISNEY WORLD SWAN AND WALT DISNEY WORLD DOLPHIN

In the heart of Walt Disney World Resort, on 300 acres adjacent to Epcot, a unique blend of sophistication and whimsy has been created in the two gigantic examples of what master architect Michael Graves refers to as entertainment architecture, the Walt Disney World Swan and the Walt Disney World Dolphin. The hotels, which opened in 1989, are located on Crescent Lake and connected to Epcot via walkways and waterways.

The 758-room Walt Disney World Swan is operated by Westin Hotels and Resorts. It consists of a main section of 12 floors and two wings of 7 floors each. The Swan features concierge service, and 52,000 square feet of meeting space, including a 23,064-square-foot ballroom and up to 31 meeting rooms. There are three restaurants, two lounges, a themed grotto pool, a game room, a fitness center, eight lighted tennis courts, and a sandy beach.

The building's exterior is painted in patterns of pastel waves, and the entire structure is showcased by giant majestic swans.

One of the crowning decorative features at the Swan is a wealth of oversized hand-painted murals displayed in every public area. Michael Graves produced small renderings for the murals, then artists followed these renderings to execute the paintings.

The Swan's sister hotel is the Walt Disney World Dolphin, operated by Sheraton Hotels. The distinctive 27-story turquoise triangular tower was honored by *Progressive Architecture* magazine. The color scheme complements that of the Swan, but instead of waves, the Dolphin features murals of banana leaves. Not to be overshadowed by a couple of big birds, the Dolphin is topped by two 56-foot-tall dolphin statues.

The Dolphin has 1,510 rooms, including 140 suites. There is a mammoth total of 202,295 square feet of meeting space. The Hemisphere Ballroom, at 55,903 square feet, is the largest ballroom in Florida, and the second largest ballroom in the country. There are also 28 meeting rooms, a boardroom, and a 51,275-square-foot exhibition hall. (Together, the Swan and Dolphin add up to the largest convention/resort complex in the Southeast.)

The Walt Disney World Dolphin features four restaurants, a cafeteria, a soda fountain, a poolside bar and grill, three lounges, a fitness club, tennis courts, boat rentals, several swimming pools, a game room, and several boutiques.

Their massive scale, eccentric decoration, and post-modern sensibilities have made these behemoth sisters very controversial among Disney enthusiasts. Love them or hate them, the Walt Disney World Swan and the Walt Disney World Dolphin are certainly, in the words of longtime Imagineer John Hench, ". . . hotels that really pull out all the stops, and work very hard not to look like hotels."

Just as Main Street, U.S.A. in the Magic Kingdom and Hollywood Boulevard at Disney-MGM Studios are not meant to represent factual history, but to evoke a collective cultural memory, the flavor of the 1920s mid-Atlantic coast is apparent at Disney's BoardWalk. The waterfront village combines an entertainment district with Disney's BoardWalk Inn and Disney's BoardWalk Villas. (The Atlantic City Boardwalk had earlier provided the decorative inspiration for the Boardwalk Candy Palace, on Main Street, U.S.A. in Disneyland Paris.)

Renowned architect Robert A. M. Stern's creation is nestled along the shores of Crescent Lake in the Epcot Resort area on a 45-acre site and includes a 378-room deluxe hotel, meeting facilities, dining, entertainment, and shopping. A 532-unit Disney Vacation Club Resort has opened as Disney's BoardWalk Villas, adjacent to Disney's BoardWalk Inn.

Already adjacent to Disney's BoardWalk Inn is a 20,000-square-foot convention center themed as a town hall, with gazebos and pavilions for intimate gatherings.

Disney's BoardWalk is the first mixed-use project at Walt Disney World, offering both hotel and residential-style accommodations, meeting facilities, restaurants, entertainment, recreation, and shopping.

Featuring colorful awnings and breezy balconies, the BoardWalk Inn and Villas sit atop a quaint collection of shops, clubs, and restaurants overlooking the boardwalk and village green. An eclectic mix of stripes and florals, fan-back wicker chairs, overstuffed sofas, and giant palms create a comfortable setting. Two-, three-, and four-story buildings surround private courtyards and manicured gardens. Additionally, there are 14 two-story garden suites, each with its own private entrance.

Hotel guest amenities include a health club, children's program, arcade, tennis courts, and themed pool. A promenade connects Disney's BoardWalk to four other Epcot Resort hotels on the shores of the lake: Disney's Yacht and Beach Club Resorts, Walt Disney World Dolphin, and Walt Disney World Swan. Walkways and water taxis connect the hotels to both Epcot and Disney-MGM Studios.

Along the boardwalk are three clubs, three restaurants, a candy shop, a bakery, and more than 9,000 square feet of shops and boutiques.

## CHAPTER SEVEN

# DISNEY'S ANIMAL KINGDOM

*I have learned from the animal world, and what everyone will learn who studies it, is a renewed sense of kinship with the earth and all its inhabitants.*

—WALT DISNEY

OPPOSITE:
*Concept painting of the centerpiece of Disney's Animal Kingdom—the magnificent, 14-story-high Tree of Life.*

People's enduring love for animals is the theme of Disney's Animal Kingdom, a new kind of live-action adventure park, which will be filled with the natural drama of life in the wild and celebrate all the animals that ever—or never—existed. On June 20, 1995, Michael Eisner announced Disney's newest and largest theme park, five times the size of the Magic Kingdom.

With a combination of thrilling rides, exotic landscapes, and close encounters with wild animals, Disney's Animal Kingdom promises to be entertaining, informative, fanciful, and fun in the tradition of all the Disney theme parks, yet it will incorporate a new dimension of reality with live animals in their natural habitats. Site preparation was nearly complete at the time of the announcement, and construction began in September 1995. Home to thousands of wild creatures, the new park will, by opening day, cover 500 acres on the western edge of the Walt Disney World property in Orange County.

The centerpiece of the park is the giant, majestic Tree of Life, 14 stories tall (nearly the height of Spaceship Earth at Epcot) and more than 50 feet wide at its trunk. Intricately hand-carved by Disney artists, the tree offers a swirling tapestry of animal forms that convey the richness and diversity of animal life on Earth. It is a powerful symbol of humankind's respect for nature.

Guests will embark on journeys into three major areas of the theme park: the real, the mythical, and the extinct.

Live wild animals and exotic landscapes set the scene for a thrilling safari that tells a dramatic story about wildlife today in Africa. Herds of live

ABOVE, TOP AND RIGHT:
*These concept drawings reveal some of the animals and landscapes planned for a safari adventure that tells a dramatic story about wildlife today in Africa.*

ABOVE, LEFT:
*Visitors will have the chance to observe life at the end of the dinosaur era.*

animals, including giraffes, zebras, lions, hippos, and elephants, will be presented in true-life adventure stories of mystery, danger and humor. As they encounter these animals, the guests will be participants, not spectators, in an adventure story in this largest land of Disney's Animal Kingdom.

In the mythical world of unicorns, dragons, and other magical creatures, guests will come face to face with make-believe animals from legends, fairy tales, and storybooks—all of which play an important role in the circle of life because of their powerful hold on our imagination. The creatures will come to life through Disney's creative storytelling.

The park's third region focuses on extinction. Guests will be whisked back 65 million years to witness the end of the dinosaur era. Disney's most advanced Audio-Animatronics will bring the giants of the Cretaceous period to life in a major thrill attraction. Other adventures will lead guests into a primeval forest and allow them to experience prehistoric life on Earth.

The foundation of this park is conservation ethics. In a commitment to worldwide conservation, Disney's Animal Kingdom has created

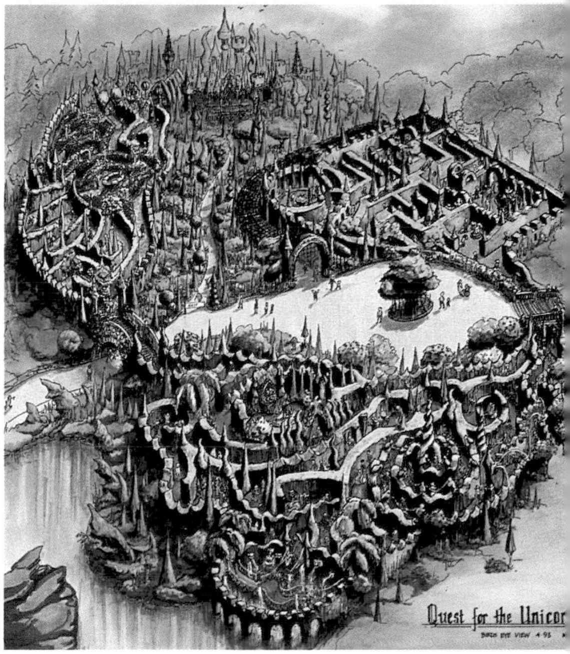


Conservation Station, headquarters for conservation and species survival activities for the park. Information on conservation organizations worldwide will help guests connect back to their own communities. Visitors can also learn about the park's Species Survival Plan program. The SSP, a program of the American Zoo and Aquarium Association (AZA), is an international cooperative breeding project, designed to manage populations of rare and endangered animals and maintain genetic diversity within species. Many of the species at Disney's Animal Kingdom will be a part of the AZA's SSP program. The goal is to inform the public about the factual importance of animal conservation and preserving their habitats and to inspire personal involvement and understanding.

The vast majority of animals for Disney's Animal Kingdom will be born in zoological parks. Others will be rescued from endangered habitats or will be orphans that have been saved by wildlife officials.

Leading the conservation efforts at Disney's Animal Kingdom is Rick Barongi, general manager of animal operations for the park. Barongi joined Disney from the San Diego Zoo, where he was director of the Children's Zoo and curator of mammals. Prior to San Diego, he served as curator of mammals at Miami Metrozoo. Barongi has a master's degree in zoology from Cornell University.

A zoological professional with 23 years of experience, Barongi specializes in the breeding and conservation of large mammals. He was involved in establishing an okapi conservation project in Epulu, Zaire. He is a professional fellow member of the AZA.

Nearly three years ago, Disney created an advisory committee, composed of the nation's leading zoologists and conservationists. This esteemed group is contributing its world-class expertise in conservation to the design and development of Disney's Animal Kingdom as well as the company's overall conservation programs. The committee has already assisted Disney Imagineers in shaping the park into a place that can inform millions about the importance of conservation through the powerful medium of entertainment. Advisors are helping shape facility designs, conservation information programs, animal management policies, and guidelines for an expanded animal conservation program.

ABOVE AND LEFT:
*One region of the park, planned after Phase One, will give "life" to the mythical world of unicorns, dragons, and other magical creatures. Guests will get a chance to see make-believe animals from legends, fairy tales, and storybooks.*

## WALT DISNEY, NATURALIST: THE TRUE-LIFE ADVENTURE

Like most of the career turns in Walt Disney's life, making live-action nature films was a completely unexpected path. Although he had brought on-screen life to animals for more than 25 years, Walt Disney himself may even have been initially surprised at such a move.

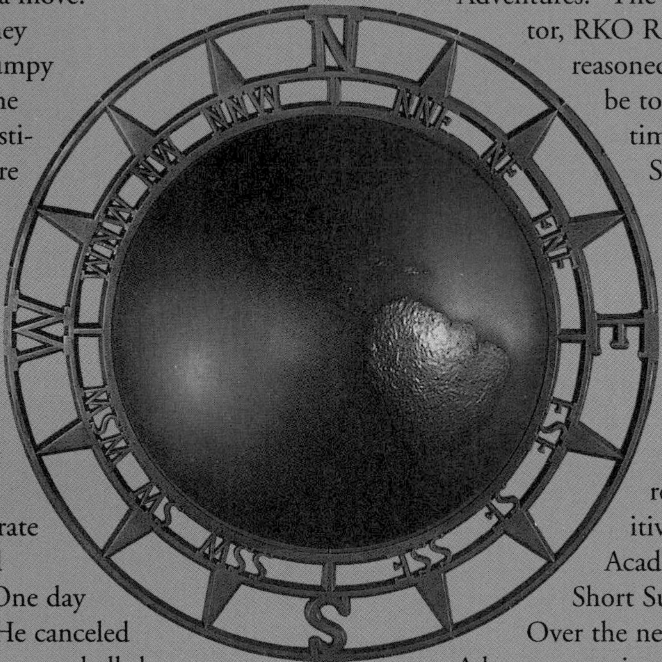


In the late 1940s Walt Disney Productions had hit another bumpy stretch in the fiscal highway. The financially comfortable but artistically unrewarding war years were gone, and the Disney brothers were looking for decisive ways to create new products. Animated features were certainly a Disney standard, but they were labor-intensive, time-consuming, and expensive.

To help his cash flow, Walt began a series of instructional industrial film shorts for corporate clients like Firestone (tires) and General Motors (hand tools). One day he shut the whole unit down. He canceled all the projects in process and returned all the advance money. Walt didn't like making this kind of educational film. If he was going to educate, it would be entertaining education, about subjects in which he was interested.

One of the subjects that interested Walt was Alaska. He considered it the last American frontier and had heard that some of the American soldiers who had been stationed there during the Second World War were going back as homesteaders. He arranged to hire a husband-and-wife team, Alfred and Elma Milotte, who had made travelogues and training and industrial films. Their instruction was vague: spend a year in Alaska photographing human and animal life—road building, mining, fishing, wildlife. The Milottes shot miles of film, which were shipped back to an editor at the studio, who sorted it by subject matter. Initially, nothing they sent back interested Walt, and he instructed the Milottes to concentrate on animals and Eskimos. The Milottes lived with the Eskimos for a year and filmed extensively in the Pribilof Islands. Walt kept tabs on the footage and was fascinated by the film of seals. In August 1947 Walt visited Alaska himself and outlined the final film: a story of the life cycle of the seals.

The result was a 27-minute documentary, *Seal Island*, the first of several films that Walt dubbed "True-Life Adventures." The film caused Walt's film distributor, RKO Radio Pictures, discomfort—they reasoned that booking the short would be too difficult, due to its running time and unusual subject matter. So Walt went to theater managers personally, securing a booking at the Crown Theater in Pasadena, California, where *Seal Island* was an immediate hit. It was then booked to run with the MGM musical *The Barkleys of Broadway* in New York City, where the critical and popular reaction was overwhelmingly positive. *Seal Island* went on to win the Academy Award for Best Two-Reel Short Subject.

Over the next decade the True-Life Adventures series continued with several films by the Milottes—*Beaver Valley* (1950, Academy Award winner, Best Two-Reel Short Subject), *Nature's Half Acre* (1951, Academy Award winner, Best Two-Reel Short Subject), *Water Birds* (1952, Academy Award winner, Best Two-Reel Short Subject), *Bear Country* (1953, Academy Award winner, Best Two-Reel Short Subject), *Prowlers of the Everglades* (1953), and *The African Lion* (1955).

Other True-Life Adventures were *The Olympic Elk* (1952), *The Living Desert* (1953, Academy Award winner, Best Documentary Feature), *The Vanishing Prairie* (1954, Academy Award winner, Best Documentary Feature), *Secrets of Life* (1956), *White Wilderness* (1958, Academy Award winner, Best Documentary Feature), and *Jungle Cat* (1959).

All in all, the True-Life Adventures won a remarkable eight Academy Awards for a series of only 13 films. Walt Disney not only invented the nature film as it would be thereafter defined, but also, in the process, enhanced his own innate interest in nature and its creatures, transforming it into a passion.

*Walt Disney meets with one of his feline stars in the introduction to a 1960s episode of* Walt Disney's Wonderful World of Color.

OPPOSITE:
*This cobalt globe was the symbol of the worldwide scope of the True-Life Adventure film series.*

Disney's Animal Kingdom Advisory Board includes:

*Karen Allen.* A principal in the Communications Office, Inc. (specializing in natural history and conservation communications), Allen has been public affairs director for Conservation International and AZA, and public relations director for the Audubon Park and Zoological Gardens in New Orleans.

*P. Dee Boersma, Ph.D.* A professor in the department of zoology and the Institute for Environmental Studies at the University of Washington, Seattle, Boersma is a research fellow for the Wildlife Conservation Society, which supports her fieldwork with Magellanic penguins at Punto Tombo, Argentina. She has recently been elected president of the Society for Conservation Biology and is a member of its board of governors.

*William Burnham, Ph.D.* President and director of the Peregrine Fund and director of the World Center for Birds of Prey, Burnham is sought out by conservation groups for advice on birds of prey. An adjunct professor at Boise State University in Idaho, he has authored some 50 scientific publications.

*Roger Caras.* President of the American Society for the Prevention of Cruelty to Animals (ASPCA), Caras is a naturalist, author, broadcast correspondent, and animal welfare advocate with a distinguished history of promoting wildlife conservation. He has written more than 60 books on domestic and wild animals and received three honorary doctorates.

*William Conway, Ph.D.* President and general director of the Wildlife Conservation Society (founded in 1895 as the New York Zoological Society),

# ENVIRONMENTALITY AT WALT DISNEY WORLD

Walt Disney World continues to be dedicated to Walt's original EPCOT philosophy of joining in partnership with organizations from around the world to test new ideas and showcase exciting projects. Research is underway at Walt Disney World to solve problems facing communities worldwide, including the growing mountain of solid waste.

Part of the solution is a concept called Integrated Solid Waste Management, summarized with three words: *reduce*, *reuse*, and *recycle*. Many urban areas have developed curbside collection and drop-off centers for recycling household trash and hazardous waste materials. In the same spirit, Disney is working on projects related to commercial recovery of pre- and post-consumer refuse. A few examples:

- Paper towels and toilet paper are purchased in jumbo rolls rather than small packages, resulting in a reduction of 813,000 pounds of packaging a year. The size of dispenser napkins has been reduced by 25 percent. This effort has decreased food service waste by 263,085 pounds per year. These two projects alone have saved the resource equivalents of more than 915 trees and 2,422 gallons of gasoline.
- The maintenance and shop areas have studied ways to reduce and reuse the chemicals and paint waste they generate. They are now utilizing a chemical cleaning unit that lets solvents be reused indefinitely. More than a million pounds of broken or surplus wood cargo and shipping pallets are collected and rebuilt or ground into garden mulch and sawdust each year.
- Infrared sensors in many restrooms and automatic irrigation controls reduce the amount of water used by as much as 50 million gallons each year.
- About 700 tons of food scrap waste are used each year as livestock feed and even more is composted.
- Each month Disney donates and delivers nearly 30,000 pounds of unserved food to a central Florida food bank that serves the area's needy.
- The Integrated Pest Management program, developed at The Land and used property-wide, replaces chemical pesticides with natural biological controls—good bugs eat bad bugs. As a result, use of traditional insecticides has decreased more than 70 percent.

I'VE GOT
ENVIRONMENTALITY
EVERY LITTLE BIT MAKES A BIG DIFFERENCE


The controlled environment of the Florida property allows Disney to analyze the waste stream and the recycling opportunities for its restaurants, hotels, retail, and business establishments and develop effective procedures to minimize waste. This information can then be shared not only within The Walt Disney Company, but, in the true spirit of EPCOT, throughout the world.

## THE DISNEY WILDERNESS PRESERVE

*Physical America—the land itself—should be as dear to all of us as our political heritage and our treasured way of life. Its preservation and the wise conservation of its renewable resources concerns every man, woman, and child whose possession it is.*

*If certain events continue, much of America's natural beauty will become nothing more than a memory. The natural beauty of America is a treasure found nowhere else in the world. Our forests, waters, grasslands, and wildlife must be wisely protected and used. I urge all citizens to join the effort to save America's natural beauty. . . . It's our America—do something to preserve its beauty, strength, and natural wealth.*

—WALT DISNEY

In April 1993 Disney extended its commitment to environmental policy when it entered into a partnership with the Florida Department of Environmental Regulation (DER), The Nature Conservancy, and five other agencies to establish The Disney Wilderness Preserve on 8,500 acres of newly acquired land south of Walt Disney World. The preserve marks the beginning of an innovative philosophy of land conservation and mitigation that embraces whole ecosystems.

The process got underway in 1991, when the Disney Development Company (then the real estate and planning division of The Walt Disney Company) completed master planning for the Walt Disney World Resort. Under state and federal regulations, wetlands lost to development must be replaced by creating adjacent wetlands of at least equal size. The DER, however, had concluded that "created" wetlands rarely survive—they are too often isolated by the development they were created to mitigate and cannot function as part of the larger ecosystem.

Working with state and federal regulators for many months, Disney modified its planned expansion to minimize any environmental impact. In a collaborative effort, Disney and the DER then created a large scale off-site wetlands enhancement, restoration, and preservation strategy in the form of the 8,500-acre Walker Ranch, south of Walt Disney World. The Nature Conservancy and Disney later rededicated the property as The Disney Wilderness Preserve. In addition, the company had earlier placed permanent conservation easements on 7,500 acres of Walt Disney World property, guaranteeing that this land will remain in its natural state.

In final form, the mitigation plan not only satisfied Disney but was also endorsed by the DER, the U.S. Army Corps of Engineers, the South Florida Water Management District, the Florida Game and Freshwater Fish Commission, the U.S. Fish and Wildlife Service, the Environmental Protection Agency, The Nature Conservancy, and other concerned organizations.

Under terms of the agreement, The Nature Conservancy will own and manage The Disney Wilderness Preserve. Disney will fund education programs, restoration activities, and management of the site. The company's total financial commitment is nearly $40 million.

In addition to its overall size and proximity to Walt Disney World, the preserve is ideal in a number of respects. Wetlands cover some 2,560 acres, nearly a third of the site. Fourteen documented and 12 unconfirmed protected species of birds and other animals are listed as living on the property, including wood storks, Florida scrub jays, gopher tortoises, and one of the largest concentrations of nesting bald eagles in the Southeast. Also, The Disney Wilderness Preserve provides connected natural areas that can function as a whole, instead of the separated island of uplands and wetlands that development usually produces.

Conway has played a leading role in the redevelopment of zoological gardens and aquariums as environmental science and conservation centers. Known as the father of the Species Survival Program of the American Zoo and Aquarium Association, he has been granted the zoological profession's highest honor, the Marlin Perkins Award. He has also received a prestigious conservation honor, the Order of the Golden Ark from Prince Bernhard of the Netherlands.

*Michael Hutchins, Ph.D.* As director of conservation and science for the American Zoo and Aquarium Association, Hutchins coordinates the conservation and science programs of more than 170 professionally managed

*A model of Disney's Animal Kingdom, with the Tree of Life toward the top right.*

zoological parks and aquariums in the United States and Canada. He is also adjunct professor at the University of Maryland's graduate program in sustainable development and conservation biology.

*John Lukas.* Currently director of White Oak Conservation Center, a private breeding preserve for endangered species in northern Florida, Lukas was previously the head biologist for the New York Zoological Society's St. Catherine's Island, off the coast of Georgia. Active in international conservation, he is president of the International Rhino Foundation.

*Terry Maple, Ph.D.* As director of Zoo Atlanta for the past 10 years, Maple has developed the facility into one of the country's premier zoos. He is also professor of psychology at the Georgia Institute of Technology and affiliate scientist at Yerkes Primate Center of Emory University. Maple is author and editor of 85 scientific publications focusing on the behavior of great apes. He was instrumental in relocating a gorilla that had been caged in a shopping mall for 25 years. The gorilla (named Ivan) was made famous in the National Geographic television special "Urban Gorilla."

*Ray Mendez.* Prior to starting his own natural history consulting business, Mendez was a scientific assistant in entomology for the American Museum of Natural History. He remains a field associate for that institution. Combining his knowledge of natural history with his talent in media, he has

worked on more than 200 television commercials and been a principal photographer for over 50 animal-related magazine articles. He has also designed numerous natural history exhibits in the United States, including the insect exhibit at the Smithsonian Institution's National Museum of Natural History.

*Russell Mittermeier, Ph.D.* President of Conservation International, an organization dedicated to field-based conservation in highly threatened, biologically rich areas of the world, Mittermeier is a world-renowned primatologist who has done extensive fieldwork in South America and Madagascar. As a leader in tropical forest conservation, he has dedicated his life to spreading the word of "the global importance of biological diversity and the fact that its loss—an irreversible process—is the most critical issue of our times."

Disney's Animal Kingdom is scheduled to open in the spring of 1998. Michael Eisner says, "Disney recognizes that the need for awareness of endangered animals and their environments never has been greater. We believe that, as storytellers and communicators, we are in a unique position to promote a deeper understanding and love for all animals. We hope that people will come here because they love animals and that, when they leave, they will have a new knowledge and respect for the beauty and complexity of the animal kingdom."

*A concept painting giving an aerial view of Disney's Animal Kingdom.*

# CHAPTER EIGHT
# ALL THE IDEAS

# WE CAN IMAGINE

*Here in Florida, we have something special we never enjoyed at Disneyland . . . the blessing of size. There's enough land here to hold all the ideas and plans we can possibly imagine.*

—WALT DISNEY

Walt Disney World continues to increase the breadth of its activities, to grow in definition, but it still remains comfortably within the context of its founder's philosophy.

The demand for resort hotel and convention space at Walt Disney World, for instance, probably exceeds the wildest visions of the people who initiated the Florida project. The number of guest accommodations on the property has grown from just 1,539 guest rooms in 1971 to a mind-boggling 20,000-plus guest rooms on site today.

## DISNEY'S CORONADO SPRINGS RESORT

Slated to open in fall 1997, Disney's Coronado Springs Resort will be Walt Disney World's first moderately priced convention hotel. The new resort will be located on 136 acres on the west side of World Drive, near the Disney-MGM Studios interchange.

Guests will find palm-shaded courtyards and elegant haciendas that provide a romantic escape from the working world. There will be more than 1,900 themed rooms and suites with Spanish-style roofs and adobe

LEFT AND OPPOSITE: *Drawings of Walt Disney World, including the Magic Kingdom at top left, Epcot with its landmark Spaceship Earth in the center, and Disney-MGM Studios just below and to the left of Epcot.*

*A model and three drawings for Disney's Coronado Springs Resort.*

walls. Eighty-one of the resort's rooms will be specially designed for the physically challenged.

For fun in the "Southwest" sun, guests can relax on the white sand beach, rent watercraft, swim in one of four themed pools, or play on one of Disney's golf courses. Other amenities will include a health club, specialty shops, dining court, lounge, and full-service restaurant.

Plentiful meeting space will be found in the hotel's 95,00-square-foot convention center, which will include a 60,214-square-foot ballroom—the largest in the Southeast. Disney's Coronado Springs Resort will be ideal for groups with trade show and exhibit requirements. More than 370 exhibit booths and 46 break-out rooms will support conventions of varied sizes. And nine loading docks will provide trucks with direct access to ballroom areas.

## DISNEY'S WIDE WORLD OF SPORTS

One of the more interesting philosophical transitions in the recent history of The Walt Disney Company was its entry into professional sports with the 1992 awarding of a hockey franchise to Disney by the National Hockey League. The Mighty Ducks of Anaheim have become another Disney success story, and Michael Eisner and his lieutenants have proved that sports can be as much a part of the Disney philosophy of entertainment as animation and theme parks. Indeed, much in the same way that Walt Disney's fondness for railroads was the starting point for Disneyland, Michael Eisner and his family's love of hockey have led to Disney's entry into professional sports.

Pursuant to the new Disney business of sports, Walt Disney World will open a complex called Disney's Wide World of Sports—a championship haven for everything from aerobics and archery to weightlifting and wrestling—on May 1, 1997.

Under construction since August 1995, some 200 acres of state-of-the-art facilities will comprise a carefully planned sports community to accommodate single-sport tournaments and multisport festivals. The complex even includes a four-and-a-half-acre town commons, where accomplishments can be celebrated with pomp and ceremony.

In its initial phase, Disney's Wide World of Sports will provide professional-caliber training and competition sites, as well as vacation-fitness facilities, for at least 30 individual and team sports. The extensive complex includes a 7,500-seat ballpark plus a baseball quadraplex, a fieldhouse that can accommodate 5,000 spectators in an arena setting around a pro-size hardwood basketball court, an 11-court tennis center with a stadium court, a softball quadraplex, beach volleyball courts, youth baseball fields, four multipurpose playing fields sized for international soccer, and a track-and-field venue.

Versatility is the key to the Disney's Wide World of Sports. More than 30 sports can be hosted in tournaments and festivals, including aerobics, archery, badminton, baseball, basketball, beach volleyball, body building, boxing, fencing, field hockey, football, gymnastics, in-line skating, lacrosse, martial arts (judo, karate, taekwondo, and others), power lifting, roller hockey, rugby, running, soccer, softball, table tennis, team handball, tennis, track and field, tumbling, volleyball, weightlifting, and wrestling.

The center also will serve as headquarters for many other sporting events taking place throughout the Walt Disney World Resort. Walt Disney World already hosts one of the nation's premier marathon races, the Indy Racing League's Indy 200 car race as well as hundreds of golf tournaments each year.

In addition, the facility will enable Walt Disney World to host more made-for-television sporting events, such as the NFL Quarterback Challenge (now held at a Disney golf course).

The 1995 Major League Baseball World Champion Atlanta Braves will make the complex its spring training home, and the Amateur Athletic Union has relocated to Orlando in anticipation of the opportunity the facility will provide for many of the more than 100 championship events that are presented by the AAU each year.

The facility promises to be visually striking. Principal architect David M. Schwarz, who created The Ballpark in Arlington, the new home of the American League Texas Rangers, has made Disney's sports community an extension of the Florida architectural neighborhood with a style he calls "Florida Picturesque."

Disney's Wide World of Sports includes the Official All-Star Cafe, a moderately priced, sports-themed family restaurant with an ownership group of such sports celebrities as André Agassi, Wayne Gretzky, Ken Griffey, Jr., Joe Montana, Shaquille O'Neal, and Monica Seles, as well as restaurateur Robert Earl. (There are already other Official All-Star Cafe restaurants, located in Cancún in Mexico, New York City, Las Vegas, and Atlantic City.) The Official All-Star Cafe is not a traditional sports bar, but a restaurant that both pays tribute to the athletes and allows every fan or aspiring superstar to relish the excitement and magic associated with sports. Disney's Wide World of Sports Official All-Star Cafe will encompass 25,000 square feet and seat 400 guests. Memorabilia from sports legends and current superstars will be displayed on the walls and in life-size cases throughout the restaurant.

The sports complex is located on Walt Disney World property in Osceola County, in an area bounded by Interstate 4 on the east, U.S. 192 on the south, World Drive on the west, and Osceola Parkway on the north.

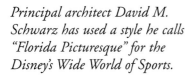

*Principal architect David M. Schwarz has used a style he calls "Florida Picturesque" for the Disney's Wide World of Sports.*

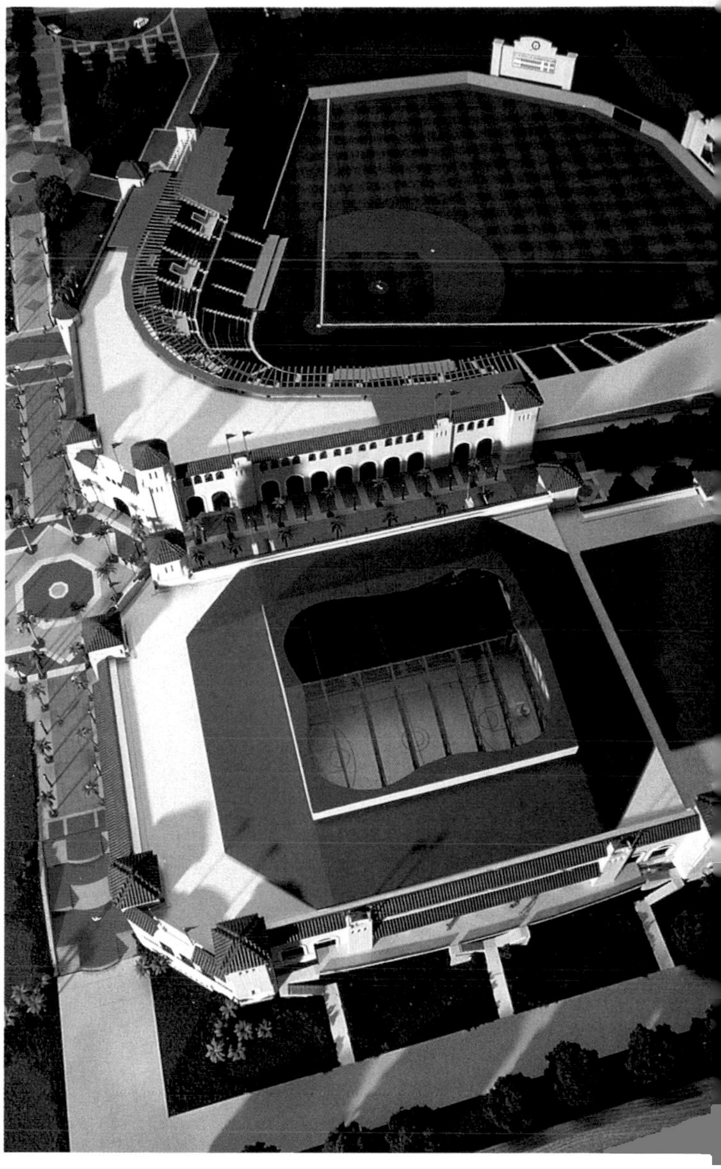

ABOVE:
*Three views of an early scale model of Disney's Wide World of Sports.*

LEFT:
*Atlanta Braves general manager John Schuerholz (left) admires the architectural model of the Disney's Wide World of Sports. With Schuerholz (left to right) are Walt Disney World president Al Weiss, Walt Disney World sports and golf senior vice president Phil Lengyel, and Walt Disney World sports vice president Reggie Williams.*

## DISNEY CRUISE LINE

Pushing the physical boundaries of Walt Disney World, as well as the philosophical boundaries of Disney entertainment, is the new Disney Cruise Line. A Disney Cruise Line vacation will be a week-long experience where guests can enjoy a three- or four-day stay at the Walt Disney World Resort followed by a three- or four-day cruise. The line's first ship, *Disney Magic,* will set sail in February 1998 and travel round-trip from Port Canaveral, Florida, to the Port of Nassau and Castaway Cay, Disney's private Bahamian island. The line's second ship, *Disney Wonder,* will set sail in December 1998.

To create the ultimate cruise experience, Disney Cruise Line commissioned Fincantieri Shipyard in Trieste, Italy, to build the two 85,000-ton, 1,760-passenger ships (based on double occupancy, with a maximum capacity of 2,400). Both ships will feature a classic exterior design reminiscent of the majestic transatlantic ocean liners of the past.

Aboard the *Disney Magic,* guests will find myriad services, activities, and programming designed specifically for families, honeymooners, adults without children, and seniors. For example, the ship will offer three themed restaurants, including the Artists Palette, designed by Walt Disney Imagineering, as well as an adults-only alternative restaurant.

The *Disney Magic* will offer the first ever seagoing entertainment program to feature Disney-created shows, activities, and special events designed for adults, families, and children. On board, the entertainment lineup includes Beat Street, an adult-oriented evening entertainment district with three themed nightclubs and a retail shop all set in a street scene atmosphere. Passengers will be free to move from venue to venue. At Rockin' Bar D they will experience a variety of live music and dancing. Bands will play rock 'n' roll and country music, including current hits and the classics, and will be augmented by top-name performers. Offbeat, the cruise industry's first shipboard comedy club, will showcase today's best comedic talent, featuring cutting-edge comedy, improvisation, and audience participation. Sessions will be reminiscent of the Carlyle Hotel in New York, where on any given evening you might find a noted pianist playing a romantic tune. Luxurious easy chairs and sofas seem at home in this sophisticated yet relaxed atmosphere.

The Walt Disney Theatre, with seats for 1,040, will offer one of the most sophisticated show settings in the world. This grand, formal theater, boasting extensive lighting and exceptional technical facilities, will showcase up to four distinct Broadway-style productions during the cruise. On any given evening, the audience can enjoy a uniquely themed production, whether a Disney classic or a newly created show that combines storytelling with music. Passengers will also have the choice of a variety of films every day at the Buena Vista Theatre, a 270-seat full-screen cinema. The fare will include Disney's animated classics and first-run releases from The Walt Disney Company's motion picture divisions.

A family lounge, Studio Sea, will offer a fun atmosphere for families with kids of all ages to enjoy. Themed after a bustling television sound stage, it will let families enjoy high-energy dance music, family-oriented cabaret acts, participatory game shows, and plenty of high-tech multimedia entertainment. The Promenade Lounge will be a perfect place to enjoy a drink with friends in a casual, drop-in atmosphere, with a live trio playing guest requests and popular standards. Sky Box Sports Club, located in the forward funnel at the ship's highest point, will offer a spectacular view. Sports fans will be surrounded by multiple screens broadcasting all the latest sports news and events from around the world.

The Disney cruise ships will feature the largest dedicated area of children's space on any ship afloat, with age-specific programming for kids ages 3 to 12, as well as a separate teen club.

Three swimming pools have been designed to create separate areas for adults, children, and those looking for a more active water experience. At night the pool areas can be transformed to create elaborate deck parties, where guests can dance under the stars on the ship's special stage.

The *Disney Magic* will feature some of the most spacious suites and staterooms at sea, 73 percent of which will be outside staterooms. More than 44 percent of the rooms will have private verandahs.

In February 1996 Disney Cruise Line acquired Castaway Cay, a 1,000-acre Bahamian island in the Abacos. Castaway Cay will be used as a day-long stop for the cruise line's two ships. Located 225 nautical miles from Port Canaveral, Florida, the home port for the *Disney Magic,* Castaway Cay is a virtually undeveloped island. Stretching 3.1 miles long and 2.2 miles wide, the uninhabited island is mainly host to transient seabirds and marine life common to the area.

Disney Cruise Line plans to create the ultimate island paradise, featuring the inherent beauty of Castaway Cay's secluded beaches, lush greenery, and natural lagoons. It will be the first cruise line to build its own private dock on an island to allow for easy access to and from the ships. There will be a half-mile-long beach area offering a wide range of water sports and beach activities for families as well as a secluded, pristine mile-long beach for adult rest and relaxation.

*The* Disney Magic, *the first ship of the Disney Cruise Line, will set sail in February 1998.*

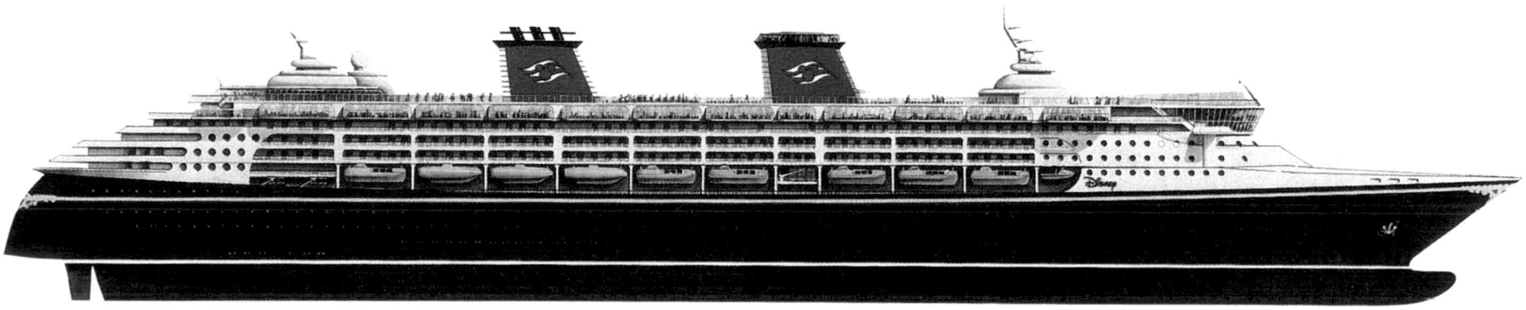

## THE DREAM CONTINUES

Walt Disney's dream for Florida was so intensely personal that it is doubtful that it could ever have been precisely realized—even by Walt Disney himself. His plans always and necessarily changed en route to reality. Had Walt lived, what he dreamed in 1966 would certainly have shifted and altered by 1971. What he envisioned in Florida was an environment for entertainment, recreation, and vacation, with a high degree of aesthetic appeal, a focus on planning, and incorporating the latest thinking of the best minds. In achieving these philosophical goals, Roy O. Disney and Walt's other corporate and creative heirs have served Walt Disney's vision well.

There are certainly still more ideas for the future of Walt Disney World on the drawing boards of Walt Disney Imagineering. New development will continue; new theme parks will be created; new attractions will open; favorite attractions will be revised, updated, and added to. Of the now 30,000-plus acres of the Walt Disney World Resort, only a total of about 10,000 acres have actually been developed. Walt Disney World will without a doubt continue growing into the next century, enlarging and expanding—as Walt Disney himself stated—"as long as there is imagination left in the world."

*A nighttime view down Main Street toward Cinderella Castle.*

# ACKNOWLEDGMENTS

I began my Disney career and had my very first trip to Walt Disney World because of Jim Cora, now president of Disneyland International. Thanks, "Uncle Jim."

Wendy Lefkon is a trusting, helpful, knowledgeable, and funny soul, and no matter what pressures she may have felt during this project, they were never transmitted to me. Wendy's editorial assistant, Monique Peterson, is a similar soul, with an energetic, helpful, and upbeat attitude. I treasure their intelligent collaboration, support, and friendship.

What would Disney do without the irreplaceable Walt Disney Archives? To my friend Dave Smith, who has supported my endeavors for the past 15 years, and to his staff—Rebecca Cline, Collette Espino, and Adina Lerner—my sincere gratitude. Dave's book *Disney A to Z: The Official Encyclopedia* was also an indispensable resource for information and fact-checking. Ed Squair at the Walt Disney Photo Archives helped enormously (and with great good humor) in the selection of historical photographs. Archivist Robert Tieman, in addition to his archival duties, functioned as personal advisor and editor—as well as a dear friend.

I simply would not have been able to research this book as efficiently as I did without the resources of Walt Disney World Information Resources at The Epcot Discovery Center—Sara Pollock, Greg Dorf, Fred Dupré, Louis Ladehoff, Steve Langlois, Reva Lee, John Naglee, Cristina Novoa, Frieda Rivera, Lori Shank, Phillip Tinkes, Ray Woelk, and particularly WDWIR staffer Lisa Newton, who assembled a gigantic package of research materials for me that proved to be a godsend.

Also at Walt Disney World, thanks to Robbie Pallard, Diane Hancock, Michael Mendenhall, and T. J. Wollard.

Tim O'Day of Disney Art Editions graciously loaned his personal collection of Walt Disney World material to me for the duration of this project. These items proved indispensable, and I promise I'll get them all back to you safe and sound, Tim. Any day now, I promise. Honest.

At Walt Disney Imagineering, my thanks to Jill Centeno, Lynne Chang, Hugh Chitwood, John Hench, Susan Hendrickson, Rick Hunt, Jean Lee, Joe Rohde, Diane Scoglio, Marty Sklar, and Eddie Sotto.

Susan Mitchell-Deitz and Ralph Kline at the Disney Development Company, Amy Foley at Disney Cruise Lines, and Dave Herbst at the Disney Sports Complex generously assisted with acquisition and clearance of the images and information used in Chapter Eight.

Jody Dreyer, vice president of Disney Corporate Synergy and Special Projects, is a supportive, helpful, and joyous person, whose combination of personal warmth and professional guidance were vital to me, although she probably doesn't know it. Now she does.

Tamara Gould at Sussman/Prejza & Co., Inc. provided extensive and helpful background on the master way-finding system designed by that company for the Walt Disney World Resort.

Thanks to Jim Babcock of The Disney Store, for his support, good humor, and infallible ability to make me laugh; to my literary agent, David Andrew; and to Ric Edinger, Betsy Richman, Dan Long, Joe Morris, Michael Pellerin, David Collins, Gilles C. Wheeler, Paul Wolski, Dave Walsh, and Gino De Young.

To my family—Grandma Mick, Mom, Ron, Jerry, and even in absentia, Dad—your support means the world to me.

Finally, very special thanks to Eddie Alexio Arturo Morales Roca.

# BIBLIOGRAPHY

## BOOKS

Beard, Richard R. *Walt Disney's EPCOT Center.* New York: Harry N. Abrams, 1982.

Belton, John. *Widescreen Cinema.* Cambridge, Massachusetts: Harvard University Press, 1992.

Bright, Randy. *Disneyland: The Inside Story.* New York: Harry N. Abrams, 1987.

Finch, Christopher. *The Art of Walt Disney: From Mickey Mouse to the Magic Kingdom.* New York: Harry N. Abrams, 1973.

——. *Walt Disney's America.* New York: Abbeville Press, 1978.

Findlay, John M. *Magic Lands: Western Cityscapes and American Culture After 1940.* Berkeley, California: University of California Press, 1992.

Fjellman, Stephen M. *Vinyl Leaves: Walt Disney World and America.* Boulder, Colorado: Westview Press, 1992.

Goodwin, Betty. *Hollywood du Jour: Lost Recipes of Legendary Hollywood Haunts.* Santa Monica, California: Angel City Press, 1993.

Gordon, Bruce, and David Mumford. *Disneyland: The Nickel Tour.* Santa Clarita, California: Camphor Tree Press, 1995.

Grant, John. *Encyclopedia of Walt Disney's Animated Characters* (Second Edition). New York: Hyperion, 1993.

Grover, Ron. *The Disney Touch.* Homewood, Illinois: Business One Irwin, 1991.

Hansford, Dee. *Gardens of the Walt Disney World Resort.* Lake Buena Vista, Florida: Walt Disney Attractions Merchandise, 1988.

Heimann, Jim. *Hooray! for Hollywood: A Postcard Tour of Hollywood's Golden Era.* San Francisco: Chronicle Books, 1983.

—— and Rip Georges. *California Crazy: Roadside Vernacular Architecture.* San Francisco: Chronicle Books, 1980.

Holliss, Richard, and Brian Sibley. *The Disney Studio Story.* New York: Crown Publishers, 1988.

Jackson, Lesley. *Contemporary: Architecture and Interiors of the 1950s.* London: Phaidon, 1994.

Jandl, H. Ward. *Yesterday's Houses of Tomorrow: Innovative American Homes 1850 to 1950.* Washington, D.C.: The Preservation Press, 1991.

Johnson, Paul C. (Supervising Editor). *Los Angeles: Portrait of an Extraordinary City.* Menlo Park, California: Lane Magazine & Book Company, 1974.

Kunster, James Howard. *The Geography of Nowhere: The Rise and Decline of America's Man-Made Landscape.* New York: Simon & Schuster, 1993.

Kurtti, Jeff. *The Great Movie Musical Trivia Book.* New York: Applause, 1996.

Maltin, Leonard. *Leonard Maltin's Movie and Video Guide 1995.* New York: Plume/Penguin, 1995.

——. *Of Mice and Magic: A History of American Animated Cartoons.* New York: Plume, 1980.

Naylor, David. *America's Picture Palaces: The Architecture of Fantasy.* New York: Van Nostrand Reinhold Company, 1981.

Passavant, Tom (Editorial Director). *Birnbaum's Walt Disney World.* New York: Hyperion and Hearst Business Publishing, 1995.

Queens Museum. *Remembering the Future: The New York World's Fair from 1939 to 1964.* New York: Rizzoli, 1989.

Santoli, Lorraine. *The Official Mickey Mouse Club Book.* New York: Hyperion, 1995.

Smith, Dave. *Disney A to Z: The Official Encyclopedia.* New York: Hyperion, 1996.

—— (Editor). *Walt Disney: Famous Quotes.* Lake Buena Vista, Florida: Disney's Kingdom Editions, 1994.

Thomas, Bob. *Walt Disney: An American Original* (First Edition). New York: Simon & Schuster, 1976.

——. *Walt Disney: An American Original* (Revised Edition). New York: Hyperion, 1994.

——. *Walt Disney World.* Lake Buena Vista, Florida: Walt Disney Attractions Merchandise, 1986.

——. *Walt Disney World: The First Decade.* Lake Buena Vista, Florida: Walt Disney Attractions Merchandise, 1981.

Zehnder, Leonard E. *Florida's Disney World: Promises and Problems.* Tallahassee, Florida: Peninsular Publishing Company, 1975.

Zukin, Sharon. *Landscapes of Power: From Detroit to Disney World.* Berkeley, California: University of California Press, 1991.

## PERIODICALS

Alexander, Kristen. "Environmental Consciousness Raising at WDI." *WDEye,* Spring 1991.

DeCarlo, Angela. "Disney's BoardWalk at Walt Disney World." *The Disney Magazine,* Winter 1995.

Disney University, The. *The Disney Team: Creating Tomorrow's Dream.* Summer 1995.

Fisher, Pam. "Today's Special: Hamburgers and Hollywood." *WDEye,* Fall 1991.

Kaplan, Sam Hall. "To See L.A.'s Past, Visit Florida." *Los Angeles Times,* February 25, 1990.

Kawamura, Steve. "Indiana Jones™ and the Imagineers' Crusade." *WDEye,* Fall 1991.

LaRue, Nancy, and Jean Lee. "Invasion of the Sci-Fi Dine-In." *WDEye,* Fall 1991.

Leerhsen, Charles. "How Disney Does It." *Newsweek,* April 3, 1989.

Okey, Anne, and Bob Laubacher. "A Tour Is Born." *Disney News,* Spring 1989.

Pasonski, Connie. "Honey, They Shrunk My Schedule." *WDEye,* Winter 1990.

Prizer, Edward L. "Disney's Biggest Gamble." *Orlando Magazine,* November 1991.

——. "Disney's 20 Years of Wonder." *Orlando Magazine,* October 1991.

——. "Inside EPCOT." *Orlando-land Magazine,* June 1980.

Rude, Suzan. "Honey, They Opened My Playground." *WDEye,* Spring 1991.

Segal, Justin. "Great Moments with Mr. Clinton." *WDEye,* Winter 1993.

Spiegel, Steve, and Jean Lee. "The Rainbow Connection: Muppets Meet Imagineers." *WDEye,* Fall 1991.

In addition, countless back issues of *Eyes and Ears of Walt Disney World* and *Disney Newsreel,* both Disney employee newsletters, were referenced in researching this book, as well as dozens of park guides, souvenir brochures, and promotional pamphlets.

# INDEX

Page numbers in *italics* refer to illustrations.